THE SHOW MUST GO ON

A COVID-19 Survival Guide

for

Performing Artists

Suzann Sime

Copyright © 2020 Suzann Sime

All rights reserved.

ISBN-13: 9798554383717

Legal Disclaimer: The information in this book is intended solely for the personal non-commercial use of the user who accepts full responsibility for its use. This disclaimer informs readers that the views, thoughts and opinions expressed in the text belong solely to the author, and do not represent the opinions of any entity whatsoever with which the author has been, is now or will be affiliated with in the future. Although the author has made every effort to ensure that the information in this book was correct at press time, the author does not assume and hereby disclaims any liability to any party for any loss, damage, or disruption caused by errors or omissions, whether such errors or omissions result from negligence, accident, or any other cause. The book is not intended as a substitute for professional advice from medical practitioners, scientists, physicians, financial advisors, accountants, lawyers, barristers and other professionals. In all cases you should consult with professional advisors familiar with your particular factual situation for examination and/or advice concerning specific matters before making any decisions.

The author and those associated directly or indirectly in anyway, cannot take any responsibility for or be held liable for things like damages that arise from reading this book and implementing any information. The chemicals listed in this book may be dangerous or even illegal in some countries and the author does not make any warranties about the completeness, reliability and accuracy of this information. Any action you take upon the information of this book is strictly at your own risk and the author will not be liable for any losses and damages in connection with the use of this book.

I would like to acknowledge Sandy Whitehouse, Sarah Finch, Alex Jones, Chloë Wennersten and Camilla Collins for their contribution to this book.

To my boys, I would not have survived COVID-19, mentally, if it were not for your love.

CHAPTER 1 Introduction	1
CHAPTER 2 A Survival Brief for Performing Artists	11
The Basics	11
Travel Companions	13
Rations	14
CHAPTER 3 Effect of COVID-19 on Castings	17
CHAPTER 4 Health & Hygiene Precautions on Set	61
CHAPTER 5 The Virus in Detail	83
CHAPTER 6 Emotional & Mental Wellbeing	99
On Reflection	109
Getting Back into Auditions	115
CHAPTER 7 Refreshing the Brand	125
Headshots	129
Social Media Photos	133
Self-taping	135
Grooming	144
CHAPTER 8 COVID-19 Wardrobe Spring Clean	149
CHAPTER 9 Rising Up Through COVID-19	157
Representation	171
CHAPTER 10 Moving Forward	185

CHAPTER 1

Introduction

The Entertainment Industry is perhaps one of the hardest hit industries worldwide during the coronavirus pandemic. With performing artists facing ongoing financial uncertainty, the unpredicted closures of venues by governments (localised and/or industry specific following the lockdown period), fluid changes in quarantine when travelling between countries, the requirement of adequate ventilation when indoors and the necessity of social distancing, (extra difficult in more confined workspaces) all make this a stressful time. Mainstream theatres will not re-open till next year, some open air theatres are doing short runs while the sun shines (though with greatly reduced audience numbers), making it challenging to break even.

In the UK, many prestigious theatres, like The Globe, gossiped about becoming a Bingo Hall or Nightclub, if not given adequate funding by government and, as we have seen, entertainment establishments over the years have become more dependant on private funding. British Arts Council programmes have been funded by the National Lottery and generous donors, and so perhaps this move to less dependency on government investment may, through this crisis, be to its detriment – social distancing being the biggest factor in safely being able to open up live venues or high-density audience cultural institutions. With that in mind, it is essential to adapt to new ways of working on set and to ensure the safety of cast and crew which will have financial implications.

Uncertainty is never a good thing for business – an obstacle for planning ahead, particularly in Opera where artists are contracted years in advance. Many artists, stage managers, designers, prop makers and directors have adapted in the meantime, finding new ways of working in odd jobs not previously envisaged, such as funeral service operators, ventilator testers, health service call centre operators, vaccine clinical trial participants, or volunteers for charities delivering food to those shielding and most vulnerable.

The effect on us as individuals, though, differs greatly; our personal experiences can fall on two ends of the spectrum and perhaps change the narrative. There are those of course that found it a pleasant time without work – able to focus on their needs and self-reflect, explore their local area, exercise more, maybe learn an instrument, catch up on movies and reading and after lockdown, take advantage of eating out with less footfall polluted environments. Yet others were, and still are, deeply concerned about contracting the virus, the impact it could have on them or their loved ones, multi-tasking, cooking three meals a day and cleaning up each time, doing the housekeeping, and homeschooling without adequate resources (as well as trying to survive), frantically disinfecting food that was delivered not venturing out even to a store, limiting areas for exercise when allowed out by government policy to avoid contact, additional pressures on social home relationships, tackling loneliness if not in relationships or with dependants, or feeling they are living as if in an open prison for months with no end in sight.

As life tries to find a way through the virus, governments globally are desperate to generate income for the long term, as this could potentially be a worse outcome than an individual contracting the virus directly. Thus, we have seen prioritising and re-starting schools (closed in the future only as a last resort) and supporting local businesses where financial districts have now become ghost towns. People have also become more complacent, not following the guidance as strictly. Hence with a lag of efficient testing in the UK, we inevitably see a rise in COVID-19 numbers. The testing becomes more efficient, suggesting we are simply picking up more cases that we had previously missed, restrictions become looser and in most countries there are fewer deaths, so this is what should be followed rather than the symptomatic cases of late. Or, then again, higher spikes but fewer hospital admissions may be attributed to the fact that younger people are infected and less likely to have fatalities, or that time and past experience has allowed the use of existing drugs, to be used for a different purpose – to alleviate the effects of the virus and reduce the mortality rate of those admitted to Intensive Care Units (ICU).

As with any severe virus, it may seem that luck itself plays a part in not getting COVID-19; reductions have not necessarily been a direct correlation to impeccable hygiene standards, as people are never 100% efficient and observant in adhering to measures. But ultimately results of any measure taken have probably been achieved by confining people to home, ensuring social distancing; thereby reducing our exposure or perhaps 'viral loading' (i.e., the amount of virus a person is exposed to), and for a while giving our immune systems time to win the fight.

COVID-19 is a virus that is transmitted from contaminated surfaces to humans, from person to person, and the latest research has also suggested that small droplets may remain in the air hours later and the virus transmitted, particularly indoors in inadequately ventilated spaces. Productions on set and in theatre have cast and crew protocols, strategies to manage the spread of COVID-19 that cover: social distancing; 'fit for work' questionnaires; travel; accommodation; trailer and unit base; catering; welfare and hygiene; costume; make up; accessing and egressing the set; on set protocol; health and safety assessments; props; sound; and, on-going testing and monitoring. No longer can cast and crew socialise and feed around the craft services table, and those artists on non-union contracts, will be treated as if, like in the USA, they are on a SAG-AFTRA (The Screen Actors Guild - American Federation of Television and Radio Artists) contract, where any actor will get their private trailer and be driven in a non-shared unit car. But these long awaited and welcomed benefits come at what cost?

In the entertainment industry there is a need to know on issues such as, "What is it like now on set?", "What precautions are in place for cast and crew health and hygiene?", "What personal responsibility does an artist need to take in the work environment?", "Is musical theatre a dying industry now?", and "What is the long term impact of the pandemic on an artist's mental health?".

Being on set will for a while look quite different: perhaps more production assistants to organise things such as hand sanitising, temperature checks and fewer technical crew, to minimise the risk and spread of infection. Calling in sick will consequently have to be taken more seriously and not simply viewed as a negative, and as most performers are freelance and only get paid when they work on set, introducing the disease to a production company could potentially spread the virus like wild fire initiated by one case, but may spark consequences that could inevitably shut down a whole production and put a lot of people out of work - a 'Catch 22' situation that begs the question - 'to quarantine or not to quarantine?'. No new production is likely be covered for COVID-19 via completion bonds or traditional production insurance. This uncertainty deters the development and production of longer-term projects which affects artists further down the food chain. Even when global governments loosen their restrictions, and filming can resume and theatres re-open in a financially viable manner, the probability of there being further waves of outbreaks until there is a vaccine or other permanent solutions could mean shutting down production companies once again, which would be too great a risk for insurance companies to ever consider.

Despite the huge growth in the creative industries this past decade, the biggest problem with any artist is that, financially, they are freelance or self-employed and their employment status is sometimes misunderstood by policy-makers; hence they can be hit hard by the current challenging circumstances. How can artists develop themselves in the meantime, what tools of the trade are worth re-investing in both time and money wise, what skills would be another string to their bow and what does the future drive in the entertainment industry look like? Is virtual reality (VR) the way of the future or more user generated content (UGC)?

It is a time to do a COVID spring clean, reassess your wardrobe, rations and branding. Most artists are out of work more than they are in work, but some performers have proved to be the most innovative and resilient people in our workforce, perhaps due to the nature and irregularity of the profession. There is, I believe, no wave too big for actors to surf. This book will attempt to explore and analyse the various ways artists can move forward and survive COVID-19 during this extraordinary time. Without a single doubt - 'the show must go on'!

CHAPTER 2

A Survival Brief for Performing Artists

'Prevention is better than cure'. This is a quick rehash of the basics and checklist: some of which may or may not be of relevance, depending specifically on the individual needs of the performing artist.

The Basics

- Avoid seeing or having any contact with people who are sick, whatever the reason.
- Get out of the habit of touching your face at home, and don't touch your face in public when your hand could be

infected.

- Sneeze into your elbow or into a tissue and discard hygienically afterwards.

- Wear a mask and encourage others to do the same, especially in confined spaces (or have a spare mask and pass it on).

- Close your social diary, stay at home, and make use of your time in different yet still productive ways.

- Join video telephony groups and socialise on video conferencing, or phone instead of face-to-face.

- Despite government advice changes, practice social distancing at all times - six feet or two meters from other people.

- Open windows for good ventilation; try to meet outside rather than indoors.

- Reduce the trips to the grocery/food store by accessing home deliveries or do a bigger shop less often.

- Allow paper or cardboard parcels to sit for a minimum of 24 hours (any plastic parcels, sanitise or discard wrapping).

- Wash hands for a minimum of 20 seconds whenever in

contact with something from outside the home, including mail/letters.

- Assume anyone outside your household, including family and friends could have COVID-19 - don't let your guard down.

Travel Companions

Anti-viral wipes.

Alcohol spray or gel (check adequate content).

Mask (additional back up).

Baseball cap (tie hair up, reduce virus aerosols on the body).

Mobile/Portable phone charger.

Phone (and back up digital device, if possible).

Emergency contacts and numbers (written down).

Pen.

Tissues (useful if prone to sneezing from allergies).

Water bottle (labelled with name).

Glasses and/or sunglasses or shield.

Rations

Dried Pasta

Rice

Passata/tomato puree

Olive oil/vinegar

Peanut butter/Vegemite or Marmite

Canned soup/beans/peas/potatoes/fruit etc.,

Crackers

Seeds

Cereal

Tea/coffee/long life milk

Chocolate

Paracetamol

Iodine/antiseptic cream or powder

Electrolyte supplement

Vitamin D supplement

Disinfectant, bleach and/or rubbing alcohol

Band aids/plasters

Thermometer

Toilet paper/Tissues

Back up of medications (e.g., extra inhalers if asthmatic)

Nail polish remover/pale polish/nail file/nail clippers

Shampoo/conditioner

Coloured dry shampoo or root concealer

Hair scissors and/or clippers

Tweezers and/or hair removal wax

CHAPTER 3

Effect of COVID-19 on Castings

During the pandemic, more than ever, it's not enough to be good - you have to be great! Don't expect work that isn't there and for the little that is, you need to be special or lucky, or both – and always prepared. And then there is timing, an additional imperative component in the formulae for success, 'being in the right place, at the right time', may no longer be relevant, as under the current conditions this ideology is severely impeded.

Social distancing requirements, the uncertainty of further lockdowns, and differences in quarantine guidelines in different countries have led to significant changes in the way casting directors (CDs… and in the USA, called casting associate or casting agent) and producers engage with talent. It has put a strain on the self-employed small- to medium-sized businesses such as theatrical agencies, because they can't simply materialise work for their clients.

Theatrical agencies are employment companies that act as an intermediary in sourcing work for performing artists that can be across the whole spectrum, covering productions that are theatrically released on the big screen, not just implying the coverage of theatre jobs alone. Depending on the country and niche of the agency, staff attached to the artist may be referred to as: agent, talent agent, talent representative or theatrical agent (and less often, booking agent). In the UK, an agent may also be called a personal manager, if they have a closer, more personalised relationship with the client incorporating career development and strategy, with the terms being used interchangeably. In the USA, though, agents and personal managers have very distinct job functions that legally cannot overlap.

CDs are now commonly asking agents to list any projects clients were attached to pre-lockdown and garnering as much detail as possible about when it was expected to shoot and any options with pick up dates etc., to enable the scheduling of artists as far in advance as possible.

During lockdown, work instantly dried up. Literally, it was like walking off a cliff. Clients anxious, stuck at home for months during lockdowns, in most cases being self-employed, were not earning and so thinking of other ways to generate an income, perhaps from their home. Voice Over (VO) work topped the number one priority for most artists as an option, particularly during lockdown, by the use of industry professional microphones which directly input and connect to a portable device or desktop editing suite – thus user friendly and more accessible to the performing artist than ever before. The internet allows for global submissions by supplying MP3/4 audio files relatively easily, using large file software solutions, such as WeTransfer or Vimeo. Commercials too took on a different slant, where home filming with a flatmate or partner or child (those living in the same household, also known as a 'bubble') were sought-after.

Additional roles not previously the norm for shoots, were advertised requesting 'back up' artists (typically used in theatre as understudies), cast via video telephony and to be 'on-call' (or 'stand-by') during the shooting period as well as preference to those artists living within the locality of the shoot. The material was then sent off for extensive editing, mostly for internet advertising rather than terrestrial usage. Theatre, film and television (TV) were as a whole put on hold, except for one or two unique productions that were close to finish pre-pandemic, those desperate to complete the series or feature film and able to adopt COVID-19 measures.

Since the pandemic's beginning, major film and TV productions, such as Netflix and Amazon, with no choice, had to reschedule and suspend shoots, of course, particularly during lockdowns. Actors' salaries were being paid for all episodes (including future contracted episodes), even those who had not completed the series, under the assumption they would resume on first call after lockdown(s) were lifted. Unfortunately, those artists in high demand were then implied first call on several productions, usually of global locations, with countries having varying quarantine rules, but scheduling a whole cast with these issues would obviously lead to further delays.

Implementation of safe work practices and personal protective equipment (PPE) has also inevitably led to lags in shoots and huge unforeseen costs. Children being homeschooled due to the pandemic further complicated issues as some artists were physically unable to find childcare, and some may also have been shielding a family member – so, working presented a difficult dilemma. And some artists with what could be seen as a somewhat manageable illness such as asthma, quite understandably felt more vulnerable. The ongoing crisis also exacerbated mental illness, many artists feeling depressed and fearful of returning to work, and some finding it difficult to obtain vital medication for ongoing conditions like epilepsy or high blood pressure due to supply chain disruptions. Productions seemed more challenged than ever: dealing with financial and personal issues was proving to be a logistical nightmare.

Theatre facing its biggest challenges with self-distancing and lockdown which meant that producers either furloughed staff if categorised as 'employed', obtaining government assistance in some countries and others paid off actors using measures such as 'Force Majeure' to end contracts. Overseas holiday resort and cruise ship productions were cancelled, essentially leaving contracted artists instantly unemployed. After lockdown, performing sectors are carrying on as best they can, and changes have had to be made to the casting process.

During virus peaks, venues for theatre are closed around most parts of the world, and there are schemes to try to continue the connection of artists with their audiences via relayed theatre websites offered up for free. Artists haven't received any income if the streaming was free and if no income was generated, although some artists in reputable theatres like The National Theatre, UK, have obtained backdated payments for live relays, receiving a share of the profits. Some theatres have moved to digital productions to raise money for the theatre. In other words, the 'show must go online'. A swift reopening of theatres seems unlikely in most cities. Keeping theatre alive seems the hardest thing to nourish during COVID-19, as with any other shared, live experience.

CDs have a commitment to inclusive, diverse casting for every role requiring agents to submit qualified performers, without regard to sex, age, ethnicity, medical condition, disability, religion, race, colour, national origin, pregnancy, marital status, gender identity, military and better status, or any other basis protected by law unless otherwise specifically indicated. Although, due to COVID-19, there has been some inference to withhold suggestions of those who are shielding or in high risk categories. In saying this, does it mean those who are older, who are generally left out on projects due to insurance restrictions at certain ages, (typically 70+ years and since COVID-19, sometimes 60+) or those with mild asthma who may be more adversely affected by COVID-19 but are normally fine, or males in the over 50s category, or certain minor ethnicities despite being on-brief, should refrain from applying for the job? This is something that the performer needs to discuss with their agent as, in any event, some overseas opportunities involving more risk may be unappealing to the artist. It is unlikely an artist would be unfairly discriminated against, and such inclusions may be more of a check for agents regarding their client being up for the task during the pandemic rather than a bias during the selection process.

More concerning are the predatory imposters, illegitimate CDs that artists need to guard themselves against. Performing artists by nature invariably tend to see the 'sunny side' of every opportunity, and so are somewhat vulnerable to what they take to be genuine offers of legitimate work, needing the guidance of an agent to assess the situation on their behalf. An agent vets the artist and should know their talent and reliability, and CDs do not like unsolicited submissions, they prefer the referral and suggestions for specific roles from the agent. Agents also know the professionalism of the CDs and the work they do, so can sift through and turn down any disreputable submissions. They will ask the right questions about projects, and double check on whether or not COVID-19 practices are in place, and make sure there are no unreasonable requests (e.g. undressing or partial nudity required during casting or self-tapes, or attending an audition alone in a hotel room) and that the venue for audition follows the recommended government guidance or industry expectations.

COVID-19 has produced a distinctive vulnerability for artists - it stands to reason that if a role seems too good to be true, it probably is. For both physical and online auditions, safety needs to be of paramount consideration. If you don't have an agent to offer advice, then you should get a friend to attend the casting with you, contact your acting union (e.g., in France this would be SFA, Syndicat Français des Artistes-Interprètes), if concerned that the casting is not being held in an appropriate and recognised work space, do your research about any audition and the company behind it. It is useful to check that the CD is registered with one of the CD international societies or guilds, but rather alarmingly some imposters have traded up on CD or others' identities. During a physical audition there should never be a request to undress or perform simulated sex acts.

I know of a case where the agent's emails were hijacked and a client was sent sides and asked to perform certain sexual acts with semi-nudity. The inexperienced artist unwittingly did this, only to be then held to ransom with threats that the material would go live unless payment received – and the whole time they did not make direct verbal contact with their agent. Since representing performing artists for over 16+ years, no CD has ever requested at an audition or on a self-tape, for a client to perform semi-naked or re-enact sexual situations, so any such requests are a clear warning sign. On the very odd occasion, pre-COVID-19, for a commercial, CDs had warned in the brief prior to the audition, that artists will need to be taped wearing swimwear and not to suggest any talent that may feel awkward doing this. These requests were made by reputable CDs and held at long-standing casting venues.

Years ago, I had a client attend an audition and without mentioning it to me, they accepted the CD's party invitation, held at their home, that evening, and to make matters worse, that artist supplied their mobile number to the CD. On reflection, the artist was unsure whether to attend but the CD telephoned them, insisting there would be some big names and great for networking. Swayed by the carrot of success, the artist attended and on arrival, realised no-one else was there yet was reassured, the others were running late. In the meantime, the CD asked the performer to improvise, first roles that were suitable and conceivable as potential future screen roles, then to explore further, try improvising animals and their behaviour, that became increasingly more embarrassing and uncomfortable for the artist. Some days later the artist confided in me. Had they informed their agent, the advice would be not to attend any private parties on their own, avoid any non-public interactions with the CD until they built up a good working relationship, particularly since they were still part of the auditioning process and, ideally, keep the relationship at a distance as they knew the CD fancied them. The artist did not want to pursue the matter further but, subsequently, I never dealt with that CD again and the artist was advised to change their mobile number. If any situation makes you uncomfortable, such as inappropriate familiarity, you should leave the room, indicate your need to ring your agent immediately and allow the agent to deal with the issues.

COVID-19 brings desperate times, but artists should continue to be selective in the jobs they audition for: an experienced actor should never do walk-on or unrecognisable work. (On the rare occasion, if the role is cut or uncredited, so the lines are cut from the final edit, this can't be helped.) In unique circumstances like the current pandemic artists could perhaps utilise their time more efficiently to learn new skills, or cash up with a paying job that is flexible and unrelated to their career, so avoiding any bad credits on their Curriculum Vitae (CV).

Low paid work could prove more costly than an artist thinks, because time is money – focusing on sub-standard performance work reduces an artist's availability for other paid work and/or auditions that are more suitable for career progression. Of course, artists do take on work for exposure, e.g., profit-share theatre, but in reality, very few professionals will find the time to attend, as with the dreaded one-person dramatic show that runs for 2 hours, self-produced and self-written.

Avoid commercials, with minuscule buyouts and in-perpetuity, which impedes artists from doing any conflicting product commercials for years, if ever. A client went for a hygiene commercial (that in those days was in the tens of thousands, today a couple of thousand as a comparison) that would only run a handful of times on terrestrial TV, so a job worth doing. On the day of the audition, the client couldn't remember the product name which was one word, two syllables, simple and well-known, they couldn't remember the short paragraph they had a week to be off page, and worst of all they couldn't remember the agent's name to whom it was related! In those days you could ring the CD, so I asked for some feedback and if they remembered actor 'X'. "Oh yes", replied one of the CDs in a sarcastic tone, explaining the situation and adding that had their advertising client been present on the day, they would have never dealt with the agency again, but on this occasion, they could only laugh and said, "with family like that, you don't need enemies."

During the pandemic, it is common to see on a brief, 'CASTING BY SELF-TAPE in the first instance and Live Zoom call back TBC' (To Be Confirmed). Or 'ONLY SUBMIT TALENT WITH SHOW REELS' which mimics requests seen on VO briefs. When the brief says, 'BY INVITATION ONLY - Do not send anything ahead', the CD isn't joking – it is as is says on the tin. When CDs say 'we will be personally asking for self-tapes', an artist needs to be patient and wait for the call. CDs are trialing many different formats: self-tapes, video telephony and online chat services like zoom that operate via a cloud-based peer-to-peer software platform. Using video telephony allows the CD to give direction in real time as opposed to obtaining a self-tape, and getting the actor to re-tape, which may discount an artist's audition as they have misunderstood the context. The problem is delays with poor internet connection (WiFi) and if the director and producer are not available at the same time, then CDs may opt for a self-tape as a better option for remote casting. If an artist is concerned about their backdrop, uploading a photo of say a landscape (remember that print will be mirror image and reversed so not image friendly unless use of other software programmes to rectify) or free stock background too is a good option.

This stresses the importance for an actor to have their tools of the trade fine-tuned – their CV, photos, show reel and voice reel all need to be up-to-date, professionally presented and stand out (for all the right reasons). Due to the high volume of out of work artists and the suspension or cancellation of many projects across the board, CDs are glancing through thousands of submissions. BBC (British Broadcasting Corporation, a government funded institution) may have five thousand submissions for one role for productions such as popular soaps like Eastenders or Emmerdale. Many artists may in fact be unsuitable due to the inexperienced agent eager to put up anyone and several clients rather than one who is absolutely right for the role, further exacerbating the selection process.

On most casting portholes, CDs see the headshot of the artists, a text box for any agent comments about the client and then need to click through to view the CV with its credit, languages, skills etc. If the artist is lucky, the CD will then click on their show reel and/or voice reel link, depending on relevance. It is a sea of faces and easy for an artist to be lost even when they are perfect for the role. CDs for any project may have to sift through hundreds or thousands of artists, so it helps if they have met them before, know the artist's work, or have booked them previously otherwise they can only make a decision on what's provided online.

If an artist doesn't have a show reel or voice reel is it the end of the world? Not necessarily, although during the pandemic where it is difficult with face-to-face auditions, reels allow for another way of knowing a person, as it serves as an interview as well as a showcase of their talents. Many CDs currently rely on reels as a basic requirement to consider an unfamiliar actor, unless their credits are impressive or talents highly suitable for the role.

Do you race out and get a show reel? Getting new content for a film or TV showreel is considered unprofessional, usually because it is with an inexperienced cast and crew, has poor clichéd script, or unsatisfactory quality and more of a quick fix – hence a fabricated show reel has never been of any use and has consequently proven to be a waste of money. Undergraduate drama student short clips do not fall under this category.

A voice reel recorded in a professional studio is useful – keep in mind that CDs want reassurance that an artist has worked in a professional environment and is comfortable working with various cast and crew, and a legitimate reel compiling of real credits reinforces this view.

The length of the show reel should be no more than three minutes, although this varies depending on the country and CD preferences; some agents say ten minutes is more acceptable, but it should be remembered that a show reel is a commercial of an artist, a vignette of different looks and roles, not a short film. CDs don't have time to view long show reels, and if they find it boring, turn off quickly – it's best to leave them wanting more. So, think of it as a concise CV; include the most recent or international material, not content from many years ago. If there is a lot of content, consider separating the material into genre and type of production – e.g., comedy or drama, and/or commercials, stage, film or TV, providing two or three short show reels a CD can peruse depending on the brief or project.

KISS (Keep It Short and Simple, or the original Keep It Simple Stupid) works; the CD wants to see you, not the other actors, not the whole story – they want to see a trailer of your varying looks and contrasting roles to show range (including accents/languages). A longer show reel can always be provided, just like a longer CV, on request or as a separate link.

Self-tapes in the past 10 years have increased in the industry, with mixed opinions. Any audition is usually taped by the CD, so whether or not the director or producer is present they have the opportunity to view the performance. It is always helpful to attend an audition in person, whenever possible, so that the actor can obtain input from the CD or ask further questions about the script/sides if not clear in how to play the character. It also serves as a 'general', a meeting which rarely exists these days unless an international artist and great credits, for the CD to find out more and keep the artist in mind for future projects.

There are also times that self-tapes have proved particularly useful. For instance, when casting in Los Angeles and the talent resides in New York; in the first instance a self-tape can help to avoid costs incurred by an artist to make the face-to-face casting, until the CD or production have narrowed down their selection for the second or third round. When artists are on set, they simply can't attend a casting, so a self-tape presents an opportunity they would not normally have access to in days when technology was not as sophisticated.

Less well-known or unknown talent have been discovered via self-tapes and taken up on jobs produced on another side of the world, so dreams do sometimes happen. However, of late, before the coronavirus hit, artists and agents had become increasingly skeptical of the usefulness of self-tapes for submissions. Artists would invariably not receive input from the CD, hence not perform at their best which could reflect on obtaining future auditions or jobs. Some CDs use self-tapes routinely as a cheaper option rather than hiring a studio space for the casting and reducing the task of having to film, edit and package the tapes for the director, as this is all done by the artist - they only need to upload or organise the links. Agents are concerned that larger numbers of artists might be asked to self-tape than would normally be attending a face-to-face casting, hence the selection process is diluted.

From a mental wellbeing point of view, artists find it stressful to be given the material the night before and then required to self-tape ASAP having to organise their own camera person/reader, edit and/or do it themselves with the added anxiety of environmental stress, such as, getting the lighting right, sound quality and pressing responsibilities or interruptions typical around the home (planes overhead, neighbours having a party, toddler having a melt-down - all just when you need to tape!).

Notably, 'hit rates' in an audition translating to a job pre-COVID were much lower when done via self-tape and the artist making the effort with little return, no input from the CD and no general. Affordable technology of high quality has helped for quicker turnarounds, but it still depends on the standard of taping the CD requires and the skills of the artist if taping themselves as to how stressful the process is, (in conjunction with preparing for the role as per normal).

The upside of self-taping is that internationally it has opened up the playing field for talent to shine and during COVID-19 allowed for artists to continue to apply for jobs remotely. Though obtaining a role and then being able to attend the shoot, are two different things. On briefs, in particular commercials, film and TV, there are reminders for agents to check their client regarding quarantine rules. Recently I had a client in Germany that had to rejoin a shoot in the UK and, at the time, there was a two-week quarantine imposed on anyone entering the country. This was not the case in Germany. A two-week shoot became an almost four-week process, because of quarantine restrictions and the increased health and hygiene precautions required on set. I felt like a table tennis ball, going back and forward between my client and the CD, trying to rearrange dates so that the actor could fulfil other filming pre-COVID-19 commitments, as well as attend new jobs and auditions. Then, the quarantine was lifted a day before their flight, job opportunities were inevitably lost. They spent the time (originally allocated to quarantine) in their accommodation, doing nothing, waiting on their call. The uncertainty meant it was still better to fly as planned rather than risk the uncertainty of being unable to fulfil the contract.

It is impossible to mitigate the risk with this unknown virus which seemingly affects people and countries differently and hence having a knock-on effect on production. On overseas jobs, agents are being told that suggested artists need to be happy to quarantine. This is where there will be the biggest effect on casting, not just internationally but regionally. There may be a regression where talent in one city e.g., Sydney in Australia, is much less likely now than ever before, to be hired on a production e.g., Neighbours, in Melbourne, in case they close the state boarders and implement quarantine. Although, this is not an uncommon practice, to promote local hire, boost business for regional communities, reduce production costs, and has worked well on supporting regional talent and productions in the UK pre-COVID-19 e.g., Dr Who in Cardiff

(Welsh natives) and TV Soap Opera Emmerdale in Leeds.

Productions based in Manchester, UK, seem to be keen to use self-tapes and video telephony as a way of casting because of the COVID-19 experience, an ability to consider actors based elsewhere without putting them at risk to the virus, by avoiding long journeys on public transport and reducing carbon footprint (this is a practice they may possibly continue with into the future).

In some instances now, production are considering various locations depending on quarantine measures e.g., shoots in Europe, may stipulate that the artists will be quarantined for seven to fourteen days on arrival in places like Kiev, Ukraine, or Tel Aviv, Israel, or the artist will be required to quarantine for five days in Sofia, Bulgaria, prior to the shoot; and be put into a hotel or apartment, given a per diem and sometimes compensated for this time before shoot, depending on contract and remembering all timelines are fluid.

The problem with COVID-19 is that in practical terms, it is uninsurable. Big production companies are able to mitigate the risk, although domestic companies more at a loss. Consequently, productions are asking for insurance indemnity schemes for a guarantee to alleviate any costs incurred for domestic TV or film productions due to COVID-induced suspension or abandonment.

Some countries, like the UK, worked during the national lockdown at the start of the pandemic to support various studios for their reopening after quarantine, by implementing rigorous testing centres on the studios, almost daily and private money available for testing as well as other health and safety procedures based on government guidance and protocols; otherwise it is estimated that around a billion pounds of production would be frozen. In the UK, there has been huge demands from online content providers, e.g., Warners Bros. and Amazon for new material, and for talent who have skills in visual effects.

There are pros and cons to the ideology, of hiring local talent based in geographical proximity to the production site. Talent will be hired more locally which is a positive change for the environment but goes against the social ideology of globalisation and 'one world, one people'. This may be fruitful for the city or town talent or country's economy, but it limits the exchange of artists. There may be a shift in productions returning to domestic studios rather than filmed abroad at cheaper locations as a way to limit risk and access the pool of talent already existent. It may lead to more unified contracts, as variations in quarantine and keeping cast and crew safe has to be agreed, which could lead to fewer pay discrepancies for wages that actors are offered on various productions, depending on its location. It may mean there are fewer productions overall, due to the cost of implementing COVID-19 safety measures, e.g. PPE and social distancing. Or lead to an increase in less site-specific filming via animation and computer enhanced productions, e.g. Computer-Generated Imagery (CGI) for green screen, crowd scenes (though this will eliminate the use of extras and walk-ons more so than actors) and shifting the use of artists required on location to avatars produced by a programmer, utilising motion capture and VO.

For animation, VO artists are being requested with the stipulation of "Please only suggest those who have HOME VOICE RECORDING STUDIOS/EQUIPMENT", though animation briefs requesting unknown voices is much less common, hence the outlay of home studio equipment and training up may not be of use when so many factors are at play. It is worthwhile for artists to discuss this with their agent before making the outlay.

During lockdown VO was in hot demand, more so by the artist than industry with audio work conducted via home studios. Most artists through lockdown have explored every artistic avenue to earn an income whilst having to be based predominately at home. Being freelance, accustomed to irregular work and highly creative, VO seems a natural progression or addition for an artist. Affordable good quality mics, user-friendly editing sound software packages and the internet has allowed far greater accessibility to VO by artists whilst at home.

There are some important considerations before investing in the kit. Firstly, is your room set up like a studio, i.e. top sound quality, cushioned walls, no external sounds (sound of the heater, an aeroplane, roommate boiling the kettle, traffic etc.), is it stereo or mono, does it have 'popping' – and, have you worked in a studio before so understand the style required (as there is very little direction)? Secondly, animation uses 'names' so celebrities or known artists are popular and now, with more actors out of work than ever before and in limbo with productions on hold, they're available! Productions favour a recognisable voice as it brings kudos to the project, which can in turn, help with funding and distribution. Thirdly, VO is a market inundated by performers, many whom are experienced in the booth, have studio set ups at home as this is what they did regularly prior to COVID-19, some have linguistic skills and can transpose, and are able to deliver the VO required with value-added skills. The VO industry is just as competitive, or more so than film and TV or stage, as it eliminates the physical so you are only judged on voice. Prices usually reflect this – a VO recording may earn a small fee as a buyout.

VO used in artificial intelligence (AI), e.g. virtual assistant AI technology, is perhaps the fastest and most convertible technology to develop and market new projects and services, compared to other 'emerging' technologies such as virtual reality (around for decades but not used widely in the mainstream). VO for virtual assistants requires endless recordings of phrase computations, though may not deliver adequately on emotions. Start-ups are behaving like stock photography companies, trying to produce a library of synthetic voice-overs, mimicking human voices, though text-to-speech technologies are far from producing a 'real life' experience, as if truly speaking or listening to a person.

Sensory is a major part of storytelling, and machine adjusted voice without inflexions or continuity of expression, produces a disjointed, unnatural experience. This is why AI is still useful more so to disseminate information and accept simple commands, and especially useful during COVID-19 to 'move to the next screen' or 'enter' so as not having to touch portable devices that are shared. Data can be recorded safely without human physical interaction.

Although a 'universal' voice does support the notion and a move in the entertainment industry for equality, 'one people' and a gender neutrality mentally, it is to the detriment of individual artists bringing character to such devices. Talent becomes defunct by use of VO computer modified libraries. This means there is no requirement for a certain voice and artificially amplifies the pool of talent, essentially increasing the supply available hence, reducing the demand and fees. The concern is, will audiences disengage if they feel they can't connect? Frustrations currently exist with virtual assistant AI technology that lacks the ability to recognise commands from non-native language speakers. AI for use in interactive storytelling (e.g. with avatars) is still not fully functional and it may take many more years before it becomes effortlessly seamless to bring to life fictional characters. Performers bring real emotions, accents, and uniqueness to characters and, for storytelling, AI will always require artists – although, as with animations, most productions will almost certainly enlist the services of a 'name'.

VO for gaming seems to be heavily reliant on the input of the director for intonation and vocal emotional expression for the various outcomes or pathways in the game. Besides compromises on the quality of the recording, gaming is multifaceted in referencing the VO data. There is a 'line' that provides a description to the programmer/creatives as a reference point (as to where it should be placed in the game, e.g. action, radio call, select option 1 or 2, cinematic introduction), then a notation of the 'intensity/volume' for vocal projection, the 'dialogue' for the artist to vocalise and finally, the 'direction' notes. Due to its abstract nature, a very clued-in director needs to be working closely with the artist and unless the artist has worked with the company previously and is familiar with their expectations and style of the project, gaining work remotely, seems unlikely.

Commercials seemed to be the second avenue that performers pursued during lockdown times as production companies were able to instruct artists at home, with their roommates or family to film on personal devices, this was edited by professionals and usually disseminated on the internet due to the quality limiting usage on big screens. Advertisers are changing their tack, searching for body-positive influencers for digital brand on online video-sharing platforms, e.g. YouTube channel or contestants for a reality TV or dating game. Brand marketers are using remote casting platforms to create UGC which is particularly suited to AVOD (advertising-based video-on-demand).

Artists are required to undertake many additional elements with a home recording that is not normally required by a performer on a commercial set, yet they are paid the same or less. As companies become leaner and unable to retain their talented workers, artists who can offer skills over many disciplines are valuable. There has always been a push towards reality TV with unpaid participants, and then advertising agencies making a push towards authenticity, with real people, real voices and experiences – which is also cheap.

Remote work seems to be the new norm when it comes to commercials or new media and UGC is one of the best tools in maintaining brand content. With all forms of video and film content, UGC has an individualistic yet holistic remote approach. Artists being both the casted and producers, it is production's way of reducing overheads, performers all within one household (bubble), avoiding COVID-19 social interaction issues. The talent is filming the content but we see them using real products, it brings an authenticity – and through COVID-19, aren't we all searching for a more real or honest world, something more we can relate to? The triple threat of the theatre; the singer, the dancer and actor extraordinaire, has now become the coronavirus evolved double threat of on-screen, that is, a talent and expert camera person.

The impact of the virus on live performances has been devastating. Some open air theatres have reopened and smaller productions are taking place, but in larger venues (replacing scheduled big budget productions, that are postponed till 2021), and weather depending as to whether the performance can confidently go forward. In addition, these productions now face the headache of distancing, PPE use, concerns of staff and changes in guidelines at the drop of a hat. On Broadway, the West End, and larger theatres finding the government guidelines impossible to make ends meet, even if they can have 50% of the seats filled, they choose not to open.

There are still online productions by reputable companies, but whether they have converted to profits in any way, or have simply been a vehicle to keep the names of the artists in the public eye, or branding for the theatre, is inconclusive. Theatre in the UK currently seems to be targeted at new graduate actors and any roles for more experienced actors are paid in line with Equity Fringe Agreement so less than minimum pay per hour for rehearsals and performances, commanding a very low fee. Larger theatres opening up, have smaller cast sizes, reduced capacity inside the auditorium and socially distanced seating so live theatre can recommence. For pantomimes (panto), CDs wanting a 'name' if it goes ahead - celebrities who tend to play these roles are the most heavily hit by the pandemic.

Whether or not productions that are heavily reliant on children performers are able to open next year when restrictions are hoped to be relaxed, is questionable as many of the headteachers of schools, e.g., UK Government schools, are demanding children and adolescents catch up on missed lesson time due to lockdown and will not allow anytime off. Some children have missed the equivalent of a term and legally, children in the UK must attend school regularly otherwise parents receive a fine and potentially criminal prosecution! This means child artists are more likely to come from schools that were pre-COVID geared to remote teaching and supportive of students to learn outside of school hours.

It is unknown when entertainers in the variety sector and circus, can perform again due to the types of venues they require, usually volumes of participants which doesn't lend well to social distancing needs. Busking may be possible, including Punch and Judy productions, if government guidelines can be adhered to. Outside venues with distancing have an advantage, weather permitting.

As productions are facing a difficult time in obtaining any insurance for the pandemic, some live events when contracting performing artists, may include COVID-19 clauses that if the contract is cancelled, there is NIL payment to the artist and, in addition, reiterate other responsibilities that the employee must undertake. Though such 'other' responsibilities are already covered by Health and Safety Work Acts or Regulations in most countries, which the employer must adhere to and hence do not need to be re-issued in a separate document, this only complicates the contract.

Artists should receive some payment in the event of cancellation against their control and this needs clarification before accepting the contract. Any dismissal of an artist should be dealt with under a production's Termination of Employment Policy which would include any COVID-19 related incident and does not need to be separately covered in the stipulations because in most countries, it is the employee's right to be treated fairly irrespective of the current pandemic's impact.

There are some government schemes to support the entertainment industries in the UK, though these tend to be more applicable to film studios like, The Walt Disney Studios and their subsidiary, Marvel Studios, all of whom are able to offer social distancing, hand sanitising stations, appropriate signage, COVID-19 tests on arrival and other necessary health and safety measures in following government guidelines, that are harder to implement in the theatre environment.

TV and film productions were suspended during the pandemic in Europe, Australasia, USA and other regions. In Germany, production for TV started up relatively quickly after their first 2020 lockdown, cast and crew changing face masks several times a day on set and safety measures in place as best as possible, hand sanitising everywhere and the opportunity for testing weekly, which other countries struggled to offer. Large productions may have hundreds of crew and cast on set and with the problems of COVID-19, the move is to stagger employees and attempt to work remotely more often. It may call for crew to multi-task for several key roles so, long term, this may affect what we see on screen.

The UK Government in August 2020 dropped the fourteen day quarantine rule with several countries which allowed shoots to resume that required overseas talent, with some still required to quarantine and others in an 'air bridge', so no quarantine required as the country of resident had lower COVID-19 numbers than the UK. In terms of new productions, besides BBC, or big studios, there seems to be a slow bounce back. Projects going ahead tend to be production companies resuming and finishing off shoots, so those companies that were covered by policies written pre-virus. Some pre-COVID-19 insurance companies, after the SARS (severe acute respiratory syndrome) outbreak did not offer such coverage, so this is dependant on each individual project. Insurance policies did not plan to cover for potential weeks of quarantine and there are upper limits depending on if it is TV or film which in real terms only offers minimal help to producers, perhaps a week maximum calculated on daily production costs.

Productions want to complete projects quickly, rewrite for social distancing, and cut any corners they would have to normally but even more so now during the pandemic. Future screen work is asking for siblings or real family members (taking up minor roles) with the chosen artist to avoid safeguarding issues of social distancing or friends whom are from the same household, they can isolate until required on set and this may reduce further setbacks going forward.

In the UK, Equity and PACT (Producers Alliance for Cinema and Television) have reached an agreement on payment where actors are asked to maintain strict social distancing prior to filming, or when there is a break in filming. Agreements might mean that actors are paid on a first call basis around £600 (August, 2020) per full week to isolate and observe social distancing during the period, if required by the producer and the artist monitored by taking antigen tests and questionnaires in relation to COVID-19, and expected to liaise with production via online rehearsals and read throughs at no additional cost.

Video games and video entertainment seem to be the least affected during lockdown as programmers and creatives can continue working from home. With augmented reality (AR), this is an application that can be used on phones and portable devices, it is a good way to present annotation, visualisation and storytelling, and particularly during COVID-19, a good way to enable online learning services for cultural institutions. It allows for digital information to be combined and overlapped on our screens whilst viewing our immediate real environment, e.g. medical industries AR to aid in seeing the anatomy of a hand, by viewing a 'real' hand on the screen, then choosing between overlapping layers that are transposed onto the screen virtually hence seeing, the circulatory system or muscles or bone configuration.

AR and virtual reality (VR) or a combination of the two referred to as mixed reality (XR) have already been used by national theatres to aid in the audiences' experience, exploring immersive storytelling with live performance. XR introduces an alternative perspective of space, whether at home or in public venues, as with a live event, and a myriad of new possibilities in ways to communicate. Smart caption glasses, e.g. used at The National Theatre in London, UK, provide users with a transcript of the dialogue and/or descriptions of the sounds of the performance on the lenses, like tiny transparent computer screens, to facilitate the experience of the audience if deaf or hard of hearing whilst viewing the performance.

During lockdown, many theatres put more emphasis into

finding live streaming content and ways of providing virtual humans as a way to communicate with those isolated whilst stuck at home. Another novel use of AR has been with Oscar gowns that can be transposed over existing photos, and a selfie in the garment taken as a keepsake, exploring various dresses and suits from several decades.

Work as a performing artist in AR is limited because social interactions generally use animations rather than physical real actors. Motion Capture (MoC) in gaming is heavily reliant on the physicality of an artist though the talents of the artists required is specific, having an understanding of stunt work or dance may help, as does theatre performance, by understanding the space when moving and speaking to add depth. If the avatar does not require a likeness to the artist, then this opens up the casting for the character, reliant more so on the ability of the performer to move in one plane as much as possible, controlling facial movements and body movements and the uniqueness of the voice.

In large green screen studios, an artist can be safely socially distanced, and cameras set up around the room, then digital data can be sent back to a processing room where programmers sit, rendering large file sizes. The same as using 360º volumetric capturing, where hundreds of cameras are set up around the presenter or dancer, or actor, who can move freely, the subject then transported to any part of the world, or scene, without travel concerns, and reducing COVID-19 exposure. This, however, requires large files of data, extensive processing times and the use of high-tech equipment.

VO for VR and AR is limited, as it tends to be driven with more well-known artists, as do conventional animations, or use of recurrent VO artists. It requires skills where an artist is able to transport themselves to that land that usually isn't visual except for a storyboard and work closely with the director in providing all of the derivations of phrases and the controller's choices in the game or story. The artist needs to be able to keep the energy and expression on abstract phrases yet keeping it real, delivering the dialogue almost the same but in a slightly different subtle way. Currently, XR does not bring more work for the artist, but focuses more on providing work for immersive scriptwriters, programmers and those in the creative industries in developing virtual sets and creating the avatar animations.

CHAPTER 4

Health & Hygiene Precautions on Set

Anyone who grew up in the 80s with AIDS, can draw a comparison with dealing with COVID-19 i.e., to assume everyone has the virus and we need to protect each other. As condoms would be handed to friends, so too should we give face masks and take precautions like keeping our distance irrespective of relaxed guidelines, as we know, 'an ounce of prevention is worth a pound of cure'.

Some 25 - 50% of people are said to be asymptomatic, though this figure may be higher depending on the country and time of data collection, and from current research even if we think we are at low risk, we must consider other beings, those in the community, at the supermarket, on the film set, at the theatre cafe, whom are more susceptible due to age, underlying health conditions, obesity and ethnicity. Even if it were a 5% chance of contracting the virus and developing lifelong repercussions or death, even those that are healthy, young and with no underlying health conditions have described contracting COVID-19 as 'living death'. Some sufferers have experienced, 'Long Term COVID', which may mean the inability to ever regain taste and smell, or feeling fatigued (still six months from the onset of the illness) or having to move back in with parents as physically unable to function as they once used to with brain fog or damage to the heart, lungs, and kidneys.

It is not just ICU or to the other extreme of just mild, there is a spectrum of complications. This is a serious game changer for those that have dependants and why, until there is a more efficient regime of testing, treating and/or vaccinating against the disease, production companies are taking a conservative approach.

Some productions require an isolation period (e.g. seven days) prior to stepping on set, even if the talent is local and there is no lockdown or symptoms, called a 'COVID testing and isolation week'. Or asked to have a test within 48 hours of stepping on set. Artists have asked if getting a test before set would speed up the procedure and open up more work avenues. The problem is accessibility to the test within a relevant time period and costs to obtain the test (and indirect fees like travelling to a distant location). Then whether or not the test is valid and accepted by production. It is best to leave it in the hands of the production company, usually the assistant director (AD) or COVID Supervisor, to organise in line with their protocols for cast and crew.

Contracts are changing and paperwork regarding increased safety measures has been put in place. Some producers asking performers to sign a waiver prior to filming so the performers acknowledge in writing that they are advised of the risks in returning to work. There should never be a blanket waiver, it needs to be specific. Artists are asked to recognise the risk posed by COVID-19, in which, despite every effort, they may directly or indirectly come into contact with the virus and they understand this risk and willingly agree to participate in the production. Under Health and Safety Law and Duty of Care in most countries, producers have a responsibility to cast and crew to adhere to appropriate safety protocols - a waiver does not negate this responsibility. Artists should not assume that the standards of Health and Safety held in their own country will be replicated in overseas lands, despite similarities. If unsure of changes in contract, artists should seek relevant union advice or that of legal professionals.

Some contracts will ask for strict social distancing prior to filming or when there is a break in filming (hiatus), and depending on whether this is TV or film, payment structures will differ, although it seems that artists should receive weekly fees during such periods. This will differ depending on union or non-union contracts and the country and/or production type. Per diems, travel arrangements, holiday pay etc., will vary for each contract. For example, in the UK, if artists are on a first call to the production and it is a part of the contractual period, then it is expected that holiday pay is calculated for each day for this entire period, whether worked or not worked, holiday pay should be paid.

Before arriving on set, artists should check the quarantine laws of that country and, in most, fill out a COVID-19 passenger locator form, this might be 48 hours before arrival in the country and is mandatory for entry. The form will require information such as the performer's passport details, carrier company name, booking reference, the name of the station, port or airport on arrival, the date of arrival, flight, train and ferry numbers, address where artists will be staying at for the first say fourteen days (this period will fluctuate), and a contact or next of kin, in case of illness.

Set productions have to do a risk assessment covering such things as filming, departments, location and cast training. This will include a protocol such as the general rules and guidance displayed in the document and production should verbally reaffirm this information at briefings to the cast and crew (sometimes via a pre-recorded video), outlining the measures that are being put place. This information will be followed up with regular meetings on site and be specific to the location and to the job. Artists will be greeted on set each day with a temperature check and asked some COVID-19 related health questions sometimes called a 'fit to work form' before given clearance and an arm band with date/clearance notice supplied to cast and crew.

It will be an individual's own personal responsibility with COVID-19 to follow the latest government guidance, both in and out of work, so this will be country dependant. Though if production wants 2 meter (approximately 6 feet) distancing yet the government only specifies 1 meter, common sense means to follow the safest of practice, within reason, and production does need to review and implement the latest government guidance, so an artist should follow protocols of production. Sometimes this will be confusing, so ask and discuss.

If social distancing can't be observed, production should implement PPE. Not only will performers need to prepare for changing quarantine rules and ways of working on set, but they will also need to make sure that on any project, in any country, they are up to speed. New guidance may include production sharing office locations and studios with multiple users. The talent and the crew need to consult with production about the correct protocol if unsure. Everyone needs to be clear on how to deal with an emergency or an incident, although priority is given to overall safety and, in this event, artists must do what they would do in a non-COVID-19 situation. Artist are asked to supply self-declaration forms and those who are at higher risk should have proper consideration, although this has a negative effect on the elderly, with some briefs stating, 'please make sure anyone you submit is not over 65, due to COVID regulations on this shoot' and this group of artists historically are already usually less employable due to insurance reasons.

Most productions, businesses and schools globally seemed to have adopted the practice of mandatory and regular temperature checks. The lack of specific symptoms of the virus and with large numbers of asymptomatic infections makes symptom-based screening difficult. It is suggested that fast testing for the virus or antibodies if widely available would help to facilitate better certainty to productions, though the evidence is not clear as yet as to the length of immunity or whether the risk of infection can be calculated using serological tests that test a person's immunity to COVID-19.

There is a huge push for temperature readings as a screening system though skin temperature can vary greatly to core body temperature, and healthy individuals naturally have fluctuations. There is little scientific evidence to support temperature screening as a reliable method for detection of COVID-19 or other febrile illness, especially if used as the main method of testing, hence it is only one component that needs to be combined with other methods.

The problem with screening by antibody testing is that if a person is tested too early in the course of the infection, their immune response may not be efficient and hence, the test will not detect antibodies. There is the use of RT-PCR, referred to as the gold-standard diagnostic test, which is supposedly 100% accurate if the sample is taken at a time when the infection can be detected, approximately five days from exposure, samples are taken from the cells or fluid from a person's throat or nose for the specific genetic sequence from SARS-CoV-2 (aka COVID-19). Not very comfortable and errors of technique can be an issue in getting a viable sample to test.

On set, artists can expect a controlled entry system, a one-way system will be set up to enter by one entrance and another separate one-way system to exit, which is currently seen in most supermarkets around the world. Interdepartmental contact has been reduced, for instance, physically separating cast and crew and communication via technology and isolating departments. Reduced numbers of cast and crew on set mean talent may have to wait until all rigging is complete and crew has cleared the floor. Designated holding areas have been allocated for artists to wait, adhering to social distancing and the number allowed in the group significantly reduced unless in a 'bubble'. This is to support combinations of people to remain together throughout the production without physically assimilating with other cast and crew, unless in the same bubble or household.

Scenes are blocked and shot to observe social distancing for all cast and crew. Employees are encouraged to work from home to reduce physical travel, via the replacement of unit or chaperon driven cars with hire cars that the artist can drive themselves. Rehearsals may constitute a zoom session when possible between the director, producer, and select performers if there is good internet access and a small enough group. Shift patterns for the cast and crew will come into place, with staggered call times further escalating the need for competent runners and assistant directors (ADs) who have good scheduling and communication skills. They will have a system response plan, a protocol to isolate if anyone is found sick at work or at home, and requirements to then test and quarantine.

Equity (the trade union for artists and creatives in the UK) has set out guidelines, where there is a risk assessment (RA) that an employer is legally required to compile. It is a catalogue of the health and safety risks and how the producer/employer intends to eliminate or mitigate these risks whilst still allowing people to get on with the job. This must be supplied to the artist before they attend the workplace and should be supplied to the agent in good time. The artist needs to have a proper understanding of the necessity of such scenes for the narrative, in advance and then have adequate time to discuss this with their agent and decide if they feel comfortable with the job and, if there are any questions, these can be dealt with before they are on set. Once the RA is finalised it is set in stone, and if, for instance, the director wants a kissing scene or any physical interaction, this needs to be then re-implemented into the RA and resubmitted to the artist and agent.

Kissing or intimate encounters are omitted wherever possible, or testing is done prior to, and the number of cast and crew are restricted on set. This has affected the type of content we see and the re-advertising of previous filmed projects. Productions are practicing social distancing on set and scripts are being rewritten to support this move, with input from the director, writer and producer, deciding whether or not certain physical interactions need to be visualised in totality or at all. Senior production determine whether an inference can be made to the romantic scene, relying more on emotional intimacy than physical, that when delivered well can be more profound. This may mean focusing on the character's reaction, or verbalising what they would have done physically, or replaying to virtual sex or sexting, or the 'after' shot of what implies that sex occurred and the paraphernalia that might have assisted that interaction, leaving the action to the audience in clever cuts, or use of silhouettes, shadows, food like grapes or other metaphorical alternatives, that narrate indirectly the sexual encounter. Alternatively, spatial positioning can be used, with COVID-19 measures in mind, a way of conveying sexual interactions without showing vivid sex scenes, e.g., where artists are back to back, rather than breathing on each other, or using quarantine for performers involved in the love scene (perhaps impractical when considering personal family commitments), or by using camera trickery with longer lenses to produce a closer sense of intimacy.

Storyboarding and committing to the shot are a time constraint for the producer in implementing COVID-19 safety measures when physical interactions are involved, so they will try to schedule intimate scenes at the end of the shoot, avoiding prior physical contact between performers. Make sure clothing, skin and hands are sanitised before and after such intimate scenes by use of food grade hydrogen peroxide. Most productions pre-COVID-19 would employ an intimacy co-ordinator to be present during rehearsal of scenes and plan for blocking and they are involved earlier now during the planning process to develop ideas.

If an artist ever feels uncomfortable, they should ask for the shoot to stop, call their agent and speak to the director. In the moment artists may feel pressured into making a decision but take time out to make the right decision. Any concerns about the scene(s), should be openly discussed for possible alternatives (including technical) and this is best discussed during the rehearsal process.

It is clear that TV and film sets will look very different for the foreseeable future. Actors restricted to their trailer and where they will be based on set. Pre-COVID, non-USA SAG (Screen Actors Guild) contracts meant sharing unit vehicles and three-way trailers on many occasions, but this has all changed and provided a more level playing field where an actor has their own trailer, necessary for all actors on all projects irrespective of the contract.

Actors will need to stay within their designated area, usually outlined with tape, chairs and tables assembled and hence should not be moved, unless directed by line managers or the head of department to complete a specific action. No visitors are allowed at the unit base, set or location. Directors or artists and chaperones (who act in loco parentis, already accustomed to observing from afar) watch the action at a distance, or remotely, so this will use more and larger monitors and megaphones, rather than direct shouting to reduce aerosols of the virus.

Social distancing from children on productions should be maintained and enquiries are directed to the designated person. If there is contact on set e.g., hugging, this should not continue off set and the child offered an age appropriate explanation of the situation and COVID-19 with ongoing support.

Animals that perform on camera may carry the virus; the transmission to humans is unclear, though stipulated can 'survive' on fur, and if touched by cast or crew can be transferred to mucosa, so contact, other than the animal with their trainer, should be avoided. Fur and hair are porous surfaces and assumed that viability is short lived; they have natural oils that protect each strand, offering some antimicrobial properties and reduce germs binding. Using shampoo, the surfactants like in washing detergent, has charged molecules that bind to virus, bacteria, dirt and oil so reduce the effectiveness of germs. Hence for cast and crew, tying the hair back (so as not to fiddle and touch the face) and wearing a cap (to protect from aerosols), if in enclosed spaces and washing the hair when returning home.

There are new systems in place to receive and send items that are used props, monitors etc., that will need to be sanitised before dispatched. Work patterns will be severely impacted by COVID-19 because productions will require more time to complete tasks – and this is one reason why cast and crew will be staggered, besides social distances measures.

Communal eating and refreshment breaks will be changed forever; distancing a major element with seating being allocated, break and mealtimes being scheduled, artists asked to bring in their own bottle (name labelled). Food will be pre-packaged and/or single servings rather than a tea point and a designated person, maybe a runner, will be in each department to collect and distribute drinks to the cast and crew. No eating or drinking on set enforced and signage will remind artists to sanitise their hands after eating or drinking. Gone are the all-you-can-eat buffet platters that staff would devour!

There will be no shared utensils and a move to single usage where artists are asked to 'bring your own' (BYO) with a one-way system and special seating layouts. Drinks and craft services will never be the same and orders placed rather than people congregating as one used to at the back of the plane on a long-haul flight having drinks with a bar service. It will not be uncommon for cast to be asked to stay within their trailer for meals. There will be communal area restrictions, so a reduction in touching surfaces (such as the fridge) with your hands and clear guidelines as to what you can do during catering and refreshment breaks, e.g. limiting the time spent with anyone and proximity, thus avoiding congregations, avoiding crowds and always practicing good hygiene.

Waste disposal are all foot operated dustbins which, to a large extent, were already in existence and clearly labelled bins for the disposal of PPE and recycling of items, e.g. utensils. All hazards are tagged and disposed of properly. Artists need to keep their area clean and tidy by using disinfectants or sanitisers and dispose of their own rubbish (including meals).

The guidance on set (in the UK) is to wash clothes at 60°C (140°F) and sanitise, meaning clean and disinfect, with detergent which will break down the virus. UK Government guidelines contradict by saying soap and water (even if at lower temperatures) will breakdown the virus. Ultimately, steam cleaning is a safer option all round, as it is less likely to damage the garment and it sanitises (but artists should always check with the Wardrobe Department and read the label instructions). All items should be clearly marked with the artist's name and performers should limit the number of personal items on set. Many productions are using fogging systems in advance of the shoot to clean and sanitise the locations, but as these chemicals settle on all surfaces and kill the virus, cast and crew are unlikely to be allowed to access the location at this time. To some, all of these chemicals used to sanitise, including fogging can exasperate certain illnesses, such as asthma.

Using action vehicles is a difficult area to safeguard. When off-camera all windows are to be opened and the minimum number of people should be used in the vehicle for the shoot. The guidance is to use remote rigs, to sanitise handles, to wash hands, to follow the government rules already in place for the public, e.g. face coverings. And then adopting appropriate hygiene practices throughout the production via single use make up or the disposal of microphone covers and to avoid sharing tools unless sanitised and no other alternatives. This includes personal items such as phones, tablet computers and chargers.

When sanitising a product, artists should check with the department to find out the correct cleaning product to use, so as not to damage equipment and make sure it is properly sanitised. Some items may be quarantined, and this is not the responsibility of the artist but something the artist should be aware of and ask questions if required.

There will be a conscious effort to reduce the number of props on set, and personal props will be left to the responsibility of the cast member. PPE should be used when in close proximity, e.g., when lifting heavy items or when putting on masks or trying on costumes or getting make up.

Cast members and costume assistants are not to access the trailer at the same time and continuity pictures to be left as is, steam cleaned costumes, on delivery to the trailer. In fact, artists are encouraged to dress themselves and bag costumes for pick up (gently place the clothes into bags rather than shaking any virus everywhere) when requiring cleaning or no longer used. Checks will be done remotely via radio communication, the microphones fitted by the artist whilst the sound team advises cast on fitting whilst observing social distancing. Only if required will sound crew assist with the appropriate PPE (gloves, face mask, apron, visor). Junior artistic directors (AD) or other crew will no longer hold umbrellas, help with coats or mind personal possessions.

When I was a runner for work experience at Channel 7 in Australia for Home and Away, I took a shine to one of the actors that was quite kind to me by not just ordering me about but actually speaking to me like a normal human being and explaining the business. As the day went on, I secretly doted on them and was at their beck and call. I even ran off to have a warm cup of tea in a polystyrene cup in my hand, waiting for them to finish their last scene for the day, until, the set lights were too hot and they threw their jumper at me to hold. At that very instance, I forgot about the tea in my hand and it went up and all over me with the jumper, that I did catch and didn't drop, though quite a bit more soggy for wear, followed by the directors loud cry, "get that work experience person out of here". I reluctantly returned to the set the next day, with my tail between my legs.

Off set, production will want to adapt the artists' journey, either by having their own private vehicle or walking or cycling to set. The use of shared vehicles needs to be properly considered if safe, with a face mask or shield worn, or a perspex wall separating the driver and passenger. Most productions in the UK are specifying a maximum of two passengers plus driver. If public transport is the last resort, artists are advised to avoid peak travel times and production will set up the scheduling to facilitate. At all times, the main idea is to maintain physical and social distancing. This is particularly difficult with international travel and any artist should not leave it to the responsibility of production but to take their own responsibility by checking local restrictions before travelling and ensure the correct face coverings and hand sanitiser are being used.

CHAPTER 5

The Virus in Detail

The virus is transmitted when people exhale and droplets land on surfaces, which other people then come into contact with. Research by the World Health Organisation (WHO) suggests the virus can be aspirated and linger in the air for 1 to 2 hours by an infected person who may be asymptomatic, usually from a laugh, sneeze or cough. This applies for singing or playing a woodwind or brass instrument, where fine droplets can be expelled at longer distances. The guidance, depending on government, when speaking normally, it is recommended that distancing is 1 or 2 meters (3 to 6 feet), the exposure is said to be limited if kept to a short time period, say 10 minutes. Singing and projecting the voice leads to the virus being spread at further distances. Dance may have the same issue, when a person is breathing more heavily, like in a gym, or a cyclist expelling more air, travelling with velocity, potentially propelling the virus in droplets further.

Research has suggested that with a cyclist or runner, particles may reach you via the slipstream. Walking at a normal pace may mean a person behind needs to stay approximately 5 meters (16 feet) in distance away, so the particles drop to the floor rather than reaching the person, and walking staggered rather directly behind may also reduce the viral loading. Wearing a mask during physical activity seems impractical as the body needs sufficient oxygen, although cyclists in busy cities routinely use some form of exhaust (neoprene or mesh cloth) valve mask – this may not be effective in protecting others against COVID-19, however.

One option is to wear shields, distance further and, when inside, safeguard with good ventilation – so any aeration of the virus suspended in the air is very quickly dispersed. Spread of the disease indoors is more of a concern, and being in the streamline of a fan may mean more intense exposure and susceptibility to the virus. Mechanical ventilation requires very high purifying uptake to be effective. During the summer of the pandemic, in France, air-conditioning in restaurants was not allowed, instead all windows were opened, and where possible, congregations outside in the open air, which was facilitated by closing of streets to provide temporary widening of pavements for more tables outside to be set up. Winter, unfortunately, doesn't support the same configuration.

COVID-19 (SARS-CoV-2, later named coronavirus disease 2019), SARS (SARS-CoV, severe acute respiratory syndrome) and MERS (MERS-CoV, Middle East respiratory syndrome) are part of the same family of viruses, called coronavirus, that causes respiratory illness and is likely to have originated in animals before being transmitted to humans by an intermediate host. The largest diversity of coronavirus is seen in bats. This type of coronavirus, one that has the ability to transmit disease to humans from animal, is called zoonotic transmission. These types of viruses that jump to a human host generally cause a serious illness. SARS-CoV seems to have originated from bats and passed onto an intermediate animal host, perhaps the civet cat, and then transferred to humans. (*But I can promise Dr. Suess, there was no cat in the hat!*).

SARS rates were far more deadly than COVID-19 although the latter seems to be transmitted more easily, as the viral load seems to be higher in the nose and throat with COVID-19. It is still uncertain if it was the pangolin (or key intermediary), seen as a gourmet delicacy (a.k.a. scaly anteater and the only known mammal with scales found in Asia and Africa), that is the intermediate for COVID-19 (i.e. passing the disease, which originated from bats, onto humans). SARS was passed onto humans by a cat and MERS spread from infected dromedary camels to people.

It is globally agreed by scientists, that wet markets (where water is predominately splashed over produce to keep cool and fresh, in an open-air market, where live and slaughtered animals are sold) have been identified as an issue because it is unnatural for specifies from different parts of the world to be in contact. Further deadly viruses will be on the increase, known as emerging infectious diseases (EIDs), if unnatural transmission between animal species, sometimes aggravated by changes in land-use including deforestation, urbanisation, and conversion to agriculture, via interaction with humans and livestock, is not controlled.

For another SARS outbreak to emerge, the virus would need to be contracted via an animal source, a laboratory mistake, biological warfare, or via untested people – hence the necessity for rapid and accurate testing regimes. Interestingly, scientists are not certain how SARS-CoV-2 spread from an animal reservoir to humans.

What all of these viruses have in common is their appearance, called Corona (which means '*crown*' in Latin), depicting the family of viruses that have spike projections on the surface that look like crowns. COVID-19 cases can range from mild to severe, while SARS cases, in general, were more severe. But COVID-19 spreads more easily. The name SARS-CoV-2 was chosen because the virus is genetically related to SARS-CoV, the coronavirus responsible for the SARS outbreak of 2003. While related, the two viruses are different. From a risk communications perspective, using the name SARS can have unintended consequences in terms of creating unnecessary fear for some populations, especially in Asia which was worst affected by the SARS outbreak in 2003, hence renaming as COVID-19 instead.

Masks offer some protection but are never 100% of the time effective against the coronavirus. Their effectiveness is dependant on the environment, whether in close proximity to the virus, like in a medical setting, and how they are worn (putting the mask on after coughing indoors or having the nose exposed is futile). The SARS-Cov-2 virus is relatively big in size compared to conventional viruses, which in turn are bigger than aromatic molecules that will penetrate the mask unless a self-contained breathing apparatus/system is used, like in scuba diving or by firefighters.

There are many different masks, including the N95 filter mask, which are designed, it is said, to filter out 95% of virus-sized particles, though smaller-sized molecules, like aromatic molecules in perfumes, will pass through. Disposable masks have a wire that sits over the bridge of the nose and needs to be sculptured correctly, to stop air flow around the gaps of the mask and focus air through the material, and should be pulled under the chin. In cheaper designs, straps are generally not adjustable though they can be crossed over to help fit to smaller faces. Exhaust valve masks, as used in cycling, do not properly protect others as the virus can shed through the valve.

For most of the population, face coverings with more than two layers of fabric such as denim, a heavy duty weaved cotton, is postulated to reduce the transmission of COVID-19 by approximately 50% or more and additional material can be used within the layering, adding another layer of filtering.

Bacteria and viruses are not the same, so anti-bacterial notations on a jar can be confusing with the contents not necessarily deactivating the virus. A virus is not living like a bacteria, which are organisms that live inside our bodies or on the skin, whereas a virus, requires a host – it enters cells and uses them to replicate itself to make more virus. Viruses are inactivated by sterilisation, good hygiene and high temperatures.

Viruses are spread when a person touches surfaces that has nasal secretions from an infected person and then touches their nose, eyes, or mouth – and the virus is able to enter the body and cause the disease, the common cold or more severe complications. Another way viruses are spread is by breathing in infected air that has droplets containing the virus when a person coughs, sneezes, talks loudly (like on mobile or cell phones), laughs, sings or has exerted breathing, as mentioned above.

Many different viruses cause common colds and there are

hundreds of different types – coronavirus is one of them. Vaccines aid in preparing and educating our immune system to recognise and combat specific infections. A single vaccine only combats one type of virus or bacteria so when there are different variants, or a new virus like COVID-19, vaccines are still being developed. In communities, vaccination works on herd immunity, so not everyone obtaining vaccination will have immunity – hence the importance of most people obtaining the vaccine, not necessarily to protect themselves but to protect society as a whole. This is the same with the pneumonia vaccine, it may help with one strain of pneumonia but not necessarily that associated with COVID-19.

The answer to the question of why the virus is more active on some surfaces and not on others is multi-factorial, depending on whether or not an envelope around the virus exists or not, the type of virus, effects on the virus regarding relative humidity, reaction to ultraviolet radiation, the type of surface (i.e. whether it is porous (paper, cloth) or non-porous (polystyrene so plastics, china, aluminium, latex)) and adsorption state (so, how fast viral particles are absorbed and immobilized, which relies on pH, electrostatic, hydrophobic interactions and/or ionic strength).

Every virus is unique and the information on COVID-19 is not yet clear. UK Government guidance says that it can live on plastics and hard surfaces (e.g., steel elevator buttons or medical equipment) up to 72 hours, on soft surfaces such as paper, COVID-19 could live up to 24 hours, and specify there is no evidence that you can catch the virus from letters and parcels. There may be no direct correlation or recorded evidence, as this would be difficult to prove, but this doesn't mean it cannot be contracted via this mode, when packaging (particularly plastics) can hold active virus for up to three days. Though if people are not following basic hygiene guidance and safe distancing, then the risk from contracting the virus from packaging, in comparison, is an almost negligible risk.

As a precaution, groceries in plastic and paper, and fresh

produce, can be left to rest for 24 hours, and packaging wiped (not the food directly as this can be toxic if ingested) with disinfectant or a soapy cloth and left to rest. Drying products aids in deactivating the virus but using a dirty cloth may mean transfer of the virus, so a disposable practice is preferable.

Common virus-positive sites are door handles, key locks, pens, light switches, TV remote controls, taps/faucets, sinks and phones. Other germ hotspots are tables, counters, kitchen cabinet handles, desks, front doorbells or buzzers (all deliveries and visitors may use this same button and it is a hard surface!), computer mouses, toilet flushes and toilets. Beware of hand dryers: the research is still out that germs can be left on hands and transferred onto the hand dryer, or dryers can suck in faecal matter and virus from aerosols when toilet lids are not closed during flushing, which then are blown around the room. Then touching the handle to leave the toilet is another red flag. Although not environmentally friendly, use a tissue and dispose of it, and sanitise hands after leaving the toilet.

The main way to combat the spread of the virus is to frequently disinfect touched surfaces daily, or make the house sacred, take your shoes off (a study found the virus can travel on the soles), leave your clothes in a pile near the front door, don't shake them to spread the virus, and wash the next day.

Many sanitisers are said to be antibacterial, but the virus is not a bacterium and then viruses are all different. In fact, using antibacterial products can encourage the development of antibiotic-resistant 'superbugs' so should be avoided. While it is not yet possible for disinfectant manufacturers to test against the exact COIVD-19 strain, the evidence is based on previous experiments on related strains of the virulent human coronavirus i.e., MERS-CoV. COVID-19 is an enveloped RNA (ribonucleic acid) virus and can be inactivated by dissolving the lipids that surround its structure using hot, soapy water (thoroughly for 20 seconds). Alcohol works in a similar way to dissolve the lipid coating, but the concentration needs to be 60% to 70% depending on the alcohol, i.e. ethanol a minimum of 63% is required and for isopropanol, a minimum of 70%. Undiluted household hydrogen peroxide (minimum of 3%) and bleach solution can also be effective. Products that claim they kill 99.9% of germs may not have the adequate chemicals or concentrations to deactivate COVID-19.

A cheap alternative is to fill a container with 7/10 of isopropyl (look on the back of packaging to see the ingredients in small print) and fill up the rest of the bottle with Aloe vera gel (the aqueous green gel not those made into creams). This addition is kinder on skin, working as a useful, cost-effective hand sanitiser. There is no need for disposable gloves unless hands are cracked or there are lesions or dryness like eczema. The skin acts as a protective barrier in itself, as long as the hands are sanitised before touching other surfaces (that need to stay hygienic) like personal possessions or the face. Disinfecting surfaces and hands can be done using high levels of pure alcohol which is easy to carry in a small spray but it's very drying if used on its own regularly on the hands, and caution, if smoking, it is a fire hazard.

Other cleaning products regularly being used with COVID-19 in the work environment include quaternary ammonium compounds (QACs), also known as quats, although the vapour may be harmful to humans, so precautions should be taken as with any toxic substance, i.e. have as much ventilation as possible – when using quats, open doors and windows at the bare minimum and wear PPE to avoid splashes that can occur. Environmentally safe cleaning products useful against COVID-19 do not necessarily mean that they are healthy for humans. To date, cleaning products containing hydrogen peroxide as the main disinfectant may be considered as equally or more effective disinfectant alternatives to quats, citric acid and lactic acid.

Alcohols may be effective, but require at least 10 minutes of full immersion/coverage (from current evidence) on certain items, which is not practical in most cleaning situations, but it does dry up on surfaces quickly – so if it's not a large work space area then it can be useful, although it's more applicable for personal items.

Fogging and spraying of entire rooms with disinfectant increases the likelihood of exposure to building occupants and is generally ineffective. Whenever possible, use of spray products should be avoided. Instead, the liquid should be poured onto a cloth to wipe on the surface. Use of quats for equipment, dishes, and other surfaces that might have contact with mouth, eyes, and other mucous membranes should be avoided. Sets and theatres should consider the use of alternative safer cleaners and disinfectants if cast and crew are in the vicinity (so best to use over weekends when spaces are unoccupied) and/or have underlying illness, that may be exacerbated.

Disinfectants are designed to be used on hard surfaces, while sanitisers are suitable for skin application. Disinfectant sprays or wipes should not be used on skin because they may cause skin and eye irritation. Many of the products approved as sanitisers and disinfectants have negative impacts on the respiratory or immune system, thus reducing resistance to the disease. In recent years, there has been a rise in evidence possibly linking asthma to the use of cleaning products and other adverse effects, like cancer of various chemicals e.g., quats and of this group, BACs (benzyl ammonium chlorides) in particular. Other compounds that may be potentially harmful include, phenolic compounds, peroxyacetic acid, chlorine compounds (e.g., sodium hypochlorite, sodium chloride, sodium chlorite, hypochlorous acid), glycolic acid, and ammonium carbonate.

At no time should a disinfectant i.e., bleach or sanitiser be ingested or injected, although there are some notable exceptions, e.g. dentists may ask to gargle with hydrogen peroxide and rinse before inspecting the teeth, but this is spat out.

CHAPTER 6

Emotional & Mental Wellbeing

It is not uncommon to have intermittent or brief physical symptoms when feeling depressed or anxious. Some of these, like feeling hot or short of breath, might make a person think they have COVID-19. This is part of the reason why there is a move by some governments to vaccinate the general population with the winter flu vaccine, so there's no confusion. This is to avoid excess numbers entering the hospital system, as well as overindulgence in testing regimes that should be specifically used for COVID-19 identification.

Uncertainty during the pandemic brings anxiety, and we

convince ourselves we have symptoms of the virus when we don't. Evaluating oneself is no easy task but there are some steps to take, such as distraction, taking deep breaths, changing the focus of the mind, speaking (though not in person incase possibly infected) to others for their perspective, and if the symptoms after evaluation are real, it is time to seek medical advice and without delay.

Performing artists tend to be the most resilient of people in comparison to the general working population, due to the nature of the business. Any long-term artist knows that CDs or agents usually have specific criteria they need to meet, whether that means adding new clients to their books or hiring, so rejection is never personal. Performers tend to be out of work more than they are working and therefore supplement their income via temporary jobs – perhaps waitressing, bar work, teaching assistant, bartender, drama coach, front of house in a theatre, ticketing, receptionist, cab or taxi driver, babysitter, museum usher, party entertainer, show reel editor, writer, programmer, and the list goes on!

Artists are used to multi-tasking and adapting to new people, roles and environments. Hence, it is not an unusual situation in terms of COVID-19 that artists find themselves having to find extra work to sustain a lifestyle. There is more stress and anxiety than normal, because there is a lot less work for everyone with the huge uncertainty within the arts sector regarding not just future work but survival of parts of the industry. This added to personal factors, since many artists are having to juggle working at home, homeschooling (or children re-starting school and the anxiety associated with increases in COVID-19 testing numbers), paying the bills whilst trying to find part-time work or re-organise finances, whilst trying to maintain their careers as a professional artist. All of this is an immense strain on anyone.

During the pandemic, artists need to discover other ways of working. Those part time jobs that used to be readily available are now in high demand. And this may continue for not just a few months, but three to five years. No-one at this time can accurately predict when we will get a handle on the virus. Now may be a time to retrain in areas that have not previously been considered. Flexible training, little outlay for equipment and remote work (useful, whether isolation is necessary or not), jobs of the future are best if they can fit around the artist.

There is a high demand in programming for VR and gaming, or AR used on desktops or portable devices, for example, Unity or Unreal offer training in C sharp and C++ training respectively. Immersive storytelling is a new area that artists would have an insightful input to, not only for the virtual sets, but also for the avatars and narration. Any job that can be a home-based occupation and obtaining the skills by learning online, deserves exploration. The problem is finding the time if stressed with family or financial commitments and it seems the less we do, the less we are motivated to do.

COVID-19 has in some instances brought out a more harmonised social cohesion, but with social distancing in place, this goes against what human beings innately find comforting. Artists want to be interactive and expressive. The pandemic has changed us all differently, perhaps even the thought of getting to set may feel daunting. When an artist steps on set, production will look and feel alien. This means that there will be fewer people on set and therefore the crew is smaller. Projects will take longer due to guidelines, and crew may be doubling up on what is needed to make a concerted effort in reducing the numbers to support social distancing measures. This is a time that productions need to think outside the box, be more resourceful, versatile – and perhaps this is where artists are best placed. This doesn't mean an artist cannot experience depression or some other mental health issue.

The press of responsibilities to get through in a day can feel consuming. It helps to write a list in priority and do just one thing every day as a start and celebrate its achievement. Staying positive is difficult as our beliefs impact on our emotions and these emotions fuel our actions. In an audition, video telephony or otherwise, sit up straight, hold your head high, stay positive, put a smile on, thus changing how the CD sees you and how you feel about yourself.

I remember a client telling me that at audition, they would go to the bathroom and take a break from the waiting space if they felt overwhelmed, groom themselves, and use their 'lucky' thing. This could be a favourite coloured lipstick, scarf or tie or perhaps, combing one's hair in a different manner, and when looking in the mirror, see the talented person reflected back. This provides a positive attitude to get through the audition. It ripples through to the CD that we have confidence and belief.

Sometimes it is difficult to ascertain what is fuelling unhealthy feelings. HOW DO YOU FEEL, really feel, inside, about friends, about life, about work, about acting, acting anywhere, any phobias, underlying health conditions, concerns about elderly relations if they are vulnerable or needing more shielding? Does performing mean the same to you now as it did before COVID-19? Do you want to move in another direction and is it as fulfilling as you thought? Can you continue to be patient with the uncertainly of the entertainment business to ride the wave, or is it already a wipe out?

It is having to be really true to yourself, the realities, your determination and beliefs to work out what will make you happy, or content, or help you change for the better. What have we learnt about ourselves and others through this pandemic? Ask others how they feel about you now – do they feel the same, have relationships shifted, have you re-prioritised your goals and aspirations in life?

This is not only important for ourselves, but for those around us. It also reflects on how positive we are when we walk into that audition, or how much effort an actor puts into a self-tape. Did we make it the best we could? It is important information to relay to your agent – they need to know how to 'sell' you and your availability both physically and mentally. This is not a time for people to be critical or judgemental, as we are all going through this journey with an unseen enemy that lives within our neighbours and friends. It has had a different impact on all of us and there is no way your agent can know how to gauge your feelings until you tell them – and thus there is the need to be clear with them yourself first.

If it takes a few days or weeks to work this out, talk to those close around, then take your time to ponder before making a response that makes you comfortable. The important thing for any human being is to have mindfulness, but pressure to make rapid decisions pushes us into impulsive, emotive and sometimes unwanted choices.

There are some coping mechanisms, like talking to someone. This seems fairly easy, but unless you know a person well you may feel better talking to someone on site about anxiety and the situation. Ensure you avoid feeling you are judged as being inadequate or less professional. In other cases, artists remain silenced over concerns they may lose their job or future work.

Whatever the situation, it is important to talk to someone,

anyone. The odd thing is, just as a little child holds back telling the whole truth to the parent, close friends and family may not feel like the right people to discuss work worries or related mental concerns. Agents are good confidents as they are expected to maintain in confidence the secrets of their clients. Of course, you will need to judge this on a case by case basis as to the existing rapport. If uncomfortable with speaking to family, friends or work colleagues, in most countries there are government anonymous online or phone help centres for mental illness. On set, there may be a COVID-19 supervisor or line manager if there are concerns regarding a colleagues' compliance. Another option is to make use of the production's employee assistance program (the artist should have been given detailed information on this) or contact the first aider.

Making good use of committed breaks away from work may aid in demoting work stresses. Use this time to have a chat with a friend over the phone on an entirely different subject or enjoy nature to get your mind off problems to provide that time out. To find five minutes in a day to be and feel IN the moment using, e.g. yoga, relaxing music, breathing exercises, meditation or reciting script. Most people tend to be more understanding than ever because they have been through at least some hardship and uncertainty or loss, and are experiencing this pandemic journey in the same time paragon as the artist.

It is always important to get rid of negativity, quiet the voices in the head and recognise problems before they become more of an issue. It is much better to share concerns and anxieties when they are first felt so they can be dealt with in a timely manner and before they snowball into bigger problems.

Again, write down all your concerns and the next day have a rethink, before putting them to production. Having time to reflect and see the issue written down could provide the solutions in dealing with the problem without having to involve others in the process. It is also important particularly for artists who are not located near or in the same country of the location for shoot to be as honest as possible about any health issues or anxiety as to why they may be reluctant or not willing to reshoot. Delaying such serious decisions is not good for the performer's mental health and it can become a huge problem for production, which helps no-one.

This is when an agent really comes into play, as a buffer between the artist and production and casting, to work out the best solution. Take advantage of your agent's expertise to help as an intermediary, to work out the best way forward if you have any concerns before production, and/or during the shoot.

On Reflection

If feeling stressed, reflect on your week. Determine, what percentage was in a stressed (or survival) zone and more in a mindful place, then change the pendulum. Identify situations that made you feel uncomfortable or those that are unpleasant and decide on ways to avoid or deal with them in the future. Engaging in actives outside of a partner or work allows for a clear mind, not multi-tasking, not trying to please others, enjoy doing something just for you.

What has been found that whatever one did before COVID-19, we tended to do more of during lockdown, whether that be eating, drinking, staying up late, arguing etc. Alcohol and drug abuse is not uncommon in the entertainment industry. The only way through addiction is by changing habits, and sometimes the habit seems worse than the physical addiction.

Eliminating the places, the people, the activities that encourages this behaviour, e.g. avoiding pubs or clubs may have helped some of us. For others, things were made worse when being forced into a lockdown situation – being deprived of physical contact, emotional support, social interaction, exercise, fresh air, nature, nurture or routine useful for motivation and stability. Then with sleeplessness, comes a vicious cycle of tiredness, eating sugar like sweets or getting it via alcohol, or high carb intake, the uppers and the downers, like coffee then alcohol, all legal and readily available, but physically and mentally damaging despite the short-lived relief. although it is hard to change habits, it is even harder to change bad habits.

There are four personality types, optimistic, pessimistic, trusting and envious. Most artists would never say they were envious, but the entertainment industry attracts an eclectic bunch of talent globally. Social media seems to be a huge trend, allowing artists to become influencers and bloggers, and to obtain large follower numbers – a necessity for self-promotion, but it is hard for authenticity, conviction and confidence when life is moving so quickly. Improving one's brand on Instagram, Twitter, WhatsApp, etc., often calls on one to answer calls instantly all day and through the night. The bright blue light from the phones and desktops further unbalances our circadian rhythm by blocking melatonin, the hormone that helps us feel ready for sleep.

Talent feels obliged to be something more than they are, to be the star of the show, but at the same time wanting to be authentic. A constant struggle and imbalance affecting emotional wellbeing, trying to reach equilibrium between the perceived and the real person. Authenticity is about presence, staying true to one's self and one's values, to have the courage to be imperfect and show what lies deep inside – although can performers really do this, allowing themselves to become vulnerable?

The experience of COVID-19 has made us all want to step away from liars, disingenuous people or big corporations that don't tailor to our individual needs. Phrases like, 'I forgot to tell you', 'sorry it slipped my mind', are now seen for what they are, a cop-out. This is not condemning 'white' lies about unimportant matters that we tell to avoid hurting others. Artists will seek a better relationship with their agent rather than just their reputation for being part of the top 10 – they want the 'Jerry McGuire' experience.

I remember being heavily pregnant and ready to pop, telling a client on a busy street in London to 'help me to help you'. I kept repeating it, over and over, almost pleading, when they didn't want to attend a very important audition because of not being keen on playing 'this' style of character. That part proved to be pivotal in their career. Artists need a solid relationship with their agent, it is a partnership. That doesn't mean you need to live in each other's back pockets but an artist needs to trust their agent's intentions and their advice, as they are tapering the work they suggest for you in line with your personal needs for whatever work that exists.

To help your agent in suggesting you for work, determine where you stand with acting now and what jobs you would commit to. Factor in those external influences around you and work out what is feasible. Trial it, can you get the nanny last minute, or groceries delivered online instead? In theory, it may seem achievable, but put into play, the impact of COVID-19 may mean there is little flexibility and support. When artists say they'll drop everything if Steven Spielberg rings, it is unhelpful for agents – the performers need to be more specific. A list an artist might find useful, may include questions such as:

- Do I want to pursue acting? - if not, then I should tell my agent (via phone or email?).

- Or am I interested in new representation? If so, why? Is this the best time to change?

- When am I ready to re-start face-to-face auditions and/or work?

- What is my availability?

- What type of work am I interested in now, commercials, TV, film, VO, gaming, stage?

- Where would I be happy to work, only locally, overseas, in certain countries, am I interested in touring?

- If I get sick overseas, who will take care of any dependants?

- How would I fund myself in a worst-case scenario if stuck in quarantine in another country, alone?

- What fee am I happy to accept on certain jobs, what minimum, or only industry accepted rates?

- Am I happy to be tested twice a week if production requires this?

- Will I self-isolate prior to shoot away from family and then on set for the full duration?

- Have I had COVID-19 (though there is no evidence if this will help immunity to the virus), does this change my decisions?
- Does my passport have more than 6 months before the expiration date?

Getting Back into Auditions

Detachment from other human beings and the entertainment industry for a long period during the pandemic, separation from the entertainment industry, inability to meet with colleagues, to do gigs and to practise the art, may mean it feels quite daunting when an audition finally comes through, particularly if it is face-to-face. Going back to doing what normally, or typically, brought enjoyment may now be replaced with anxiety. A call from the agent may not be gleefully received and excuses regarding the audition or unavailability or other commitments, anything rather than the truth or venturing out into that space again.

That's why it is important for artists to explain to their agent and be clear on exactly what types of work they feel comfortable with, rather than finding fault in the role because it is too clichéd, or it isn't the right career move – but stop procrastinating, ask why not? If it is a fear of getting back to work despite addressing all the other concerns, work out if it is a fear of failure, or rejection, or dissatisfaction about your body? There is probably no good reason for the anxiety.

Doing an appraisal and asking others that you trust for their perspective can supply understanding which is always a comfort. Even seasoned artists may always have some 'butterflies in the tummy' trembling, sweaty palms – the thing is, to what extent and does it cause long term or significant emotional, mental and/or physical damage. Excitement and anxiety are initiated in the brain, as does any emotion, both are arousal states of the mind and the body, providing identical feelings that encourage performance and action, though we will interpret them differently as to whether they are productive and welcomed. Both reactions can elucidate the same intense physiological response and by flipping the mental state from anxiety (worrying thoughts and tension) to exhilaration (an overflow of happiness), this provides a positive mental experience.

Going into audition with a positive and confident demeanour reinforces or changes our moods into positive actions. Keep telling yourself how excited you are because the reality is, it is exciting when artists do what they love. Focus on the process not the outcome, have fun and think of the benefits. You're doing a workshop with a respected CD and you are building your networks, even if not for this role, for the future, it is a win-win situation.

It brings artists back to the notion of preparing and practising the role properly. The importance of mindfulness, being in the moment, allowing time for our practical mind to process the information and not act impulsively when experiencing extreme emotions. Emotions allow us to act, which can be a proactive initiator in certain situations, though sometimes it may be an illogical progression. Artists can free their minds by taking the decisions on how to play the character and being committed and accepting of that choice, before the audition, thus less likely to be overwhelmed in making the right changes when emotions run high.

Professional artists are off page before any audition, are dressed to impress (in attire suitable for the role, though this does not need to be extreme, for if unsuccessful, it may feel awkward and embarrassing, particularly if it is a grass skirt in the middle of winter!). A taste of the character e.g., shirt, a scarf, or hat, hairstyle or colour can give enough to the imagination and feel of the character. It is vital to have a good attitude. If a face-to-face audition, try to reduce any stress associated in problems locating the casting suite, by leaving earlier to get to the venue (usually arriving an hour before), do a reconnaissance (informally referred to as a 'recce'), then have a tea or water (caffeinated coffee can lead to the jitters!) and rehash over the notes. Or read, be it a newspaper, a joke book or lighthearted quotes, which tend to alleviate stress levels without an artist becoming too absorbed in the story and forgetful of time!

When people are stressed, they tend to be less conscious of time and things go wrong – for example, planning out the car journey to get to an audition, even doing that trip prior to the day, leaving ample time factoring in traffic, yet on the day of the audition panic because of some traffic convinces the artist to go against the plan, disagreeing with the satellite navigational system and taking all but the right routes like some maniac in a F1 Grand Prix. I have experienced this situation first hand, it was scary and the driver in a trance, not listening to any reasoning and subsequently 10 minutes late for the audition. I advise clients when in an unfamiliar area and lost, if possible, to hail a cab/taxi, as spending a bit of money to get to the audition in time without the stress, is worth it.

When entering the casting suite, this is the moment to turn off or mute all calls and alerts on the phone, which tend to increase irritability and agitation, not useful before an audition (or music or drama exam). Electronic devices can be distracting and contradictory to being in the moment. Artists should arrive and register approximately fifteen minutes before their time and they can ask if the schedule is running on time, another good reason to have a book, or to review the sides if long delays. One last stop to the bathroom, any final touches, a sip of water (not too much to be running back to the toilet) and take a break, relax and sit down if possible.

Some artists find it useful to have a general chat with those waiting, but be careful whom you choose. Perhaps best to go for those that are dissimilar, so you aren't competing for the same role. Nothing is worse to bring down an artist's confidence than a bragging artist (and no-one wants a shouter in a closed space in near proximity during COVID-19!). Comments like, "I have a high calibre, well-known international representative…", "did you attend that audition last week for that top new TV programme?", or "who's your agent?… are they a new agency? I've haven't heard of them.", tend to make you doubt both your agent and your ability. Statements such as, "I have years of experience and this is just another day, no biggie", is meant to boost their own confidence.

I remind clients that the entertainment industry does not always tell the truth, it is filled with embellishment and talking a good game. The volume of castings does not necessarily correlate to the quality of the work those artists boast about. Sometimes artists can attend 20, 30 or 50 auditions before a hit (so the audition converting to a job), so I have been told. This number may reflect on the artist's ability, but it could be an indication that the roles they are suggested for are unsuitable and should be more streamlined. A hit rate is dependant on many factors: physicality, talent, competition and the number of roles available for an artist's individual specification, so a good agent will put this into perspective. They know the steps to move forward or evaluate realistically. From personal experience, a good hit rate for an accomplished and in demand actor is around 1 in 3 targeted auditions and a 'pencil' (the CD putting an artist on hold for the job, thus shortlisted with other candidates for the same role) means little – as it is unclear how many artists are in the same situation and these days, tends to be used as a backup for reserves.

When entering the room, have a smile, remember to tell yourself you're great, you're a winner, and this will be fun! Engage in the introduction with the CD and/or panel. Centre yourself in the space. Take a breath and be authentic. When we are in our own mental space, time seems to be longer than in real time. Taking twenty seconds may feel like a minute, hence the urge to rush to start. Don't do it! The CD is probably still doing work/set up whilst you are getting in the right mental state. Then do it - 'real'. BE the character, deliver the sides, and don't ACT. Don't focus on being verbatim, but carry on and deliver. It is the ESSENCE the CD is seeking.

Artists can ask if they may try again if unhappy with their performance, otherwise wait for the CD's instruction. The CD will usually guide an artist towards a delivery more in line with the director's notes. If no response, you could offer up an alternative way to portray the character (make sure you understand why you have chosen this interpretation if asked). Whether or not the CD wants this could be because they are truly happy with your previous performance, or time is tight, or for no reason at all, they have simply seen enough – so don't over think and leave happy.

Preparation is key to making decisions on how to play the character. Can you play it smaller, provide contrasting portrayals of the character that still work, more jovial, or with more aggression, showing more fear? Can you tone it down a hundred-fold? Playing with the piece may open up options, not originally thought of, that feel plausible. Then decide based on the context, which portrayal to go with.

When the CD sees your audition, they may ask for it to be done in a different way. By practising the character with a myriad of emotions and interpretations, an artist should be prepared and fell comfortable in delivering this instantly and with commitment. The same goes with singing, in particular musical theatre. Try to play with the lyrics and give the character depth, even if subtle contrasts. It is always good to try to get a coach, an expert in the field to comment on your decisions and work through it, polish and re-evaluate although not necessarily a convenient time during the pandemic to organise last minute. Perhaps self-taping and getting their views from a distance is still better than nothing. Then follow up with a video telephony dummy audition/workshop.

CHAPTER 7

Refreshing the Brand

Use this time to do some housekeeping where you re-evaluate your look, your CV and how CDs see you on acting portals (essentially a photographic actors' directory), where agents and CDs communicate, e.g. Actors Access (Breakdown Services), USA, Spotlight, UK, Showcast in Australia and New Zealand, or Stagepool used in Scandinavia and Germany. Parts of Europe have government agencies that support actors and use other portals. Look at your 'competitor' to see why they are doing well and to see how you fit into the market.

Define what your unique selling point (USP) is and perhaps integrate this into your overall appearance and outlook. Know who and what you are selling. Don't provide too many options, make sure it is succinct, simple and play to your strengths. Make sure your brand is clear across all channels: casting profiles, headshots and show reels and social media (if used), so people choosing you will feel secure in their choice. Make sure your look is solid and confident, and attend to any personal maintenance, grooming a priority.

During lockdown, artists' appearances have changed. Normally a performer should speak to their agent before making any major changes e.g., haircut, hair colour, tattoos, new beard or moustache or their removal. Agents should know the trends for casting or have a 'hunch' and be able to advise accordingly. Ultimately, it is the performer's decision. Shaving one's head, even though a radical choice, might be something that could earn money, e.g. hair growth advertisement, or epic TV drama, or used for a good cause, like a charity info-commercial.

Not being able to attend hairdressers, in some countries for months, made us appreciate how much a bit of pampering can improve our day, not just our overall general look. For self-tapes and any audition, being groomed, hair, nails and attire, even if it is for a grungy role, is imperative. A messy look on camera can be accentuated and be too OTT (over the top) in a bad way. The CD is always observing, deciding if the artist is professional, perhaps by picking up on little details such as manicured hands that aren't going to be on camera. During the pandemic, CDs will cut artists some slack, though there are ways to keep up a decent level of grooming at home cheaply.

Perhaps one of the most difficult issues for an artist is determining their playing age. Many a client has said they can play ten years younger, and I agree, in theatre that is perhaps correct, on certain high school productions like 'Grease', or if playing a child (but the audience accepts you are in fact, an adult playing down) or in comedic roles. Although even when a person looks youthful for their age, as soon as they are in a casting room amongst those ten years younger, in general, you look your age. It's not just about not having wrinkles, it is also other minor changes in body shape, muscle tone, eyelids, that as a whole create an age.

Human beings have always sought the elixir of life, dyed hair to cover grey, Botox to get rid of lines and the like and in the entertainment industry, to be appealing to younger markets and be given more of the lead roles that tend to be for younger artists. Maturity is inherent and shows through despite the best intentions of an artist. Though this idea is changing and there are more roles for older artists.

Accept your biological age and work with a plus or minus of six years at most. It is unlikely any artists would go for the older age! For children there is usually a lot less leeway. Work it out and then use that age when dressing for headshots, auditions, and watch TV and films for artists who are in a similar age group for their choice in hair styles and attire. This will allow CDs to see you in roles that you are more likely to land. If pretending to be thirty and are in your mid-fifties, the CD will be confused as to why the agent has sent you in.

Headshots

Artists always ask agents, who can they recommend to do headshots, but I find this difficult. The experience is very different from one artist to another, therefore I ask that they do their research with fellow artists and reputable photographers. Look at their shots and decide if that fits how one wants to be portrayed. Getting up-to-date headshots is an investment in your career.

During the pandemic, this may be difficult so if your look has changed, getting an outside headshot using natural light against a brick wall or plain background may be useful as an additional shot amongst your online portfolio, but get this independently reviewed. Some CDs do headshots and clients have sometimes been drawn into this service, so they also get to meet the CD. Keep in mind, is the CD someone reputable and worth having as the photographer, because their name will be credited on every headshot on the casting portals and more importantly, do they take a good shot?

You only need a few good headshots, to show various looks and expressions. A serious face on every shot does not convey much or having the face slightly tilted to the one side in the same position is boring (although asymmetry helps to hide imperfections, like one eye being bigger than the other, as does smiling with the tongue beneath the top teeth to elongate the chin and face). Having three hundred photos to go through isn't necessary, nor are several wardrobe changes. If it is a refresh to update your portfolio, then an outdoor light session with the photographer for one to two hours, is sufficient, though in-studio shots do provide a different feel.

If you have used a good photographer before with whom you had good rapport, why change the formulae? Stay with the professionals who you feel the most comfortable with and who bring out your personality through your eyes. It isn't all about the 'name'.

An experienced artists' photographer will provide the

appropriate input though some main points are:
- It should be 'natural' and an accurate representation of how you look,
- Grooming is important, including nails and eyebrows, even if going for a rugged look it needs to be styled,
- Appearance should be as neutral as possible. A CD wants to see the 'real' you, your personality and range of expression,
- Around five good head and shoulders shots showing range and one full length shot is useful,
- Blurry, pixelated or amateur photography makes an artist look unprofessional and deters CDs,
- Wear something simple (no logos/prints), v-neck or round neck, fitted/tailored clothes,
- Focus on the subject, so avoid props, hats, distracting backgrounds and accessories (e.g., earrings that are too distinct),
- Eyes are the most important feature, so make sure they are as visible as possible.

Dressing in vibrant colours helps an artist to stand out amongst the crowd and, on younger people, brings out their youthfulness – although choose solid colour tops without distracting patterns. Taking three tops, perhaps with contrasting necklines and colours, that complement the artist (tops with sleeves seems to be more flattering for most rather than cut off sleeves, tank top styles). For a different look, artists can add a tailored jacket or denim jacket worn over the top. Clothes should be crisp and wrinkle free so bring them on hangers or fold them carefully. It shows that the artist is polished and means business!

When you have gone through your shots, make a short selection, maybe twenty that are your favourites, and forward the link to your agent. Sometimes the photographer can forward the entire roll to your agent, but it is a good idea to choose some to bring to their attention rather than having to peruse the whole lot from the get-go. Agents are professionals and they know exactly what CDs are looking for, so work with them and trust their judgment.

Different countries will have different styles. In the UK, black and white photos are still used in theatre, and are more easily replicated in black and white print photocopies, in the USA, shots can be more flamboyant, then it becomes subjective. With digital cameras, a good photographer will be able to offer both colour and black and white photos during a session.

Social Media Photos

It is useful to have photos taken at a premiere, with the logos behind reaffirming an artist's credentials. Even better if they are taken with a well-known celebrity or respected director, in terms of marketing. It is often tiresome to obtain photos from the professional photographers for use as promotional material. Sometimes organisers can't find those specific photos or have deleted them, sometimes the photos are unattractive as the production's preference is focussed on marketing the other cast member who was in the photo who has a bigger name, or the photos cannot be released.

I remember at a London independent film festival, taking photos of my client and the director as well as having asked for the professional shots, in which, for some, I was included. On receipt, I could not believe from the four photos I was in, just how bad I looked, was my dress really that ghastly?! But when I then looked at photos I had taken of the director and compared shots, they too looked terrible! The only one that looked great was the lead and my client who looked OK, so that was fine for publicity of the artist, but I would never showcase any of the photos that included me.

The biggest problem with professional photos is that the photographer owns the copyright. The artist must be granted permission to be able to use the photo of themselves and sometimes this can cost money to buy the license and/or usage can be restricted or come with caveats, such as embedded advertising if used on websites. This is when your agent adds value at the premier, and not your partner, as it is a business networking event as well as an opportunity to get some good photos. Your agent can promote and do the introductions around the room, whilst at the same time, take photos on the red carpet or the personal shots backstage on press night.

It is advisable that artists take selfies whilst on set, as giving your phone to someone to take the shot doesn't automatically mean you own the rights – contracts would need to be in place to be 100% certain. It is good practice to obtain photos with the director and cast, as well as on your own, to avoid any upsets if the other talent do not want to be actively publicised with the artist. Then it is easy to take down the 'group' photo and replace with the lone artist, whilst respecting and keeping good relations with the cast and crew.

Self-taping

Self-tapes allow for greater reach and coverage of artists (particularly whilst face-to-face castings are challenging due to restrictions), exploring new talent and taking more risks, as there aren't the hard constraints of only being able to see a certain number of tapes during a time slot. Most of the casting industry agrees that during COVID-19 it is an important and sometimes essential first step (or only option as video telephony has its own problems largely due to internet connectivity).

Some CDs use self-tapes rather than show reels to assess new talent, unbeknownst to them, because show reels may not portray the actor's ability accurately if done on small budgets or with bad script, or the CD is unsure of the role they are playing. A show reel can be a useful tool only when done professionally and properly edited from good quality work, hence a CD may prefer to see the artist self-tape in the actual role, with the right accent and tone of character as this takes the same viewing attention overall, so it may be a more efficient use of their time.

Keeping in mind that a self-tape may not just be for this particular role, it may be used as a mental archive by the CD for future work. A self-tape needs to be professional in appearance at the very least. To start, artists should properly research the role and production. This means searching the internet for the background, cast and crew and, if possible, watch the TV show or past films. The same is true for musical theatre productions.

Having a proper understanding of the story, the theme, tone and style is essential. Every production will have a different idea of the characters, they may come across more warmly even if a villain, or in a comedic production the artist should play it dry, there will be a certain pace and rhythm. CDs are looking for the next new talent to not only bring the role alive in a natural manner but to also arrange the individual artist, like a flower, with the other performers to create a beautiful bouquet.

Any audition, whether it is face-to-face or a self-tape, should be effortless and, unless told to do it slapstick or OTT, actors should play it small, nuanced and not confuse a stage performance with that for camera where the audience will be up close and personal. The best screen actors seem to do super-subtle movements with their eyes and face to convey the story and this is what makes them believable in the role. There are very few actors that can be a chameleon across all styles of acting from musical theatre, to straight theatre, to film and TV, and gaming, that those that can are a rare commodity.

A performing artist can practise by putting themselves on tape, viewing it the next day, deciding if it is believable and/or emailing self-tapes to peers who will tell the truth and provide good constructive criticism. Sometimes a performance needs to be toned down a hundred-fold and can be OTT on the first practice, hence it is not uncommon to do several takes before satisfied – tiring, but essential to get it right. Keep your attire on brief. Plain garb is better than shirts with logos or dizzy patterns. Remove any prominent jewellery. If you don't have any, invest in some cheap plain tops or clothes, and jeans seem to fit universally (as the tape is focused on the head to rib-cage) but no holes. Solid colours like blue and green work well – choose something that compliments your eyes or colouring.

When clients go on holidays, Murphy's Law they will get a

good audition. I had a client who went to the middle of the wilderness, somewhere in the mountains of Eastern Europe, where the wolves howled and the bears wandered, and him telling me it was a place I would love, when I hate spiders and snakes growing up near a creek in Australia. He had nothing but a couple of t-shirts, no shaver, poor reception and hadn't had a haircut for weeks so not only did he struggle in uploading the self-tape, but he had no attire to suit the role of business man and it was a leading role. So take a few items, a tailored jacket, plain t-shirt, coloured t-shirt (two contrasting colours), day dress and little black dress, just items that could suit many different looks and go for fitted clothes, if a plunging neckline, perhaps hold out on the short shorts, or vice versa.

If you require new clothes, factor in time delays and the inability to try them on in-store, depending on the government guidelines. During COVID-19, ordering online has increased significantly but sees approximately 50% of clothes returned. Choosing from existing brands that you have previously owned/own and using the same sizing with reduce the amount of returns on new garments purchased online. Many actors don't pay enough attention to the lighting or their costume for self-tapes – again, you don't need to dress OTT but make sure your shirt, hair or skin doesn't match the background (choose a neutral homogenous backdrop).

There is plenty of good information about self-taping on the internet and on CDs websites. Do your research on lighting and sound. Spend the time to fine tune your audition technique. Understand the brief, the CD's instructions for the self-tape and be off page. The more familiar an actor is with the sides, the more natural and effortless the performance. Rehashing the main points:
- Place the camera (mobile device) on a stable foundation or tripod, positioned at eye level, filming in a landscape for a 'close up' (framed slightly above the head and bottom of the rib cage) filling 2/3 of the frame with your image and the other 1/3 where you might be speaking to the other character (known as a standard single shot set up for film)

and ensure you have an eyeline with the character you are speaking to by using a prop as a substitute for focus, then a 'thinking spot' to break eye contact could be somewhere just behind the camera but at the same eyeline as the reader.

- For the ident (slate), it is a short intro where you state your name, name of the role, agent (if applicable), and height, then your profile (a full body shot, then to turn to the left, hold, back to front, turn right, hold and back to front), and include any other information the CD has asked for, maybe shots of your hands, or a quick summary of past roles that may be relevant, e.g., if the role requires other languages/accents, you could try introducing yourself by using both your native language/accent and the language of the role. Some CDs may not want an ident and instead prefer a non-verbal full view body shot at the end of the self-tape. It is all subjective so read the instructions and follow them always.

- Light must be good enough to see your eye colouring and daylight is the best, whenever possible. The light should come onto the wall where the artist is positioned, so positioned opposite, not directly above, not sideways and not from behind, the idea is to stop shadows.

- Noise is a big consideration. Most phones today and tablet computers are great at getting the sound up close so make sure the camera person and/or reader, is not speaking loudly as their voice is closest to the microphone. This is a common problem. If the speaker has a strong accent this can influence your accent or take away the focus. If auditioning for an American production, finding a reader/camera person to bounce off your American accent really helps. Listen for background noise both inside and outside of the house such as traffic or birds tweeting and think of better spaces or times to tape.

- Get another person to read the other character's lines if possible (the 'reader'), or worse case, use a remote reader via video telephony or as an absolute LAST resort, record your own voice of the lines on a digital device to play back during the self-tape by leaving gaps for your 'live' audition role lines. Talking as if one person by reading all the roles is somewhat confusing, though using a device with a previous recording can offer a slight change in the voice to seem as if a reader. Prior taping of your voice and using this replay during the self-tape, portraying the other characters, somehow does make a difference.

- When shooting multiple scenes, some CDs want all the scenes together, with the introduction included, others don't mind if sent independently via a link e.g., WeTransfer depending on file size. Actors always ask "which one should I send?". If unsure, send two to your agent for them to make the decision. Only one take on the sides is what a CD wants, you need to remember they have hours of self-tapes to go through so be committed to what you think is best, and/or your agent, and send in your top choice. Quality is important, though balancing the upload time required to view the self-tape counts and self-tapes are usually seen on a screen smaller than a TV (so 4K becomes cumbersome for the user). Some cloud-based online platforms allow for the transfer of different types of files for free to other internet users BUT may not allow for your video to be downloaded at the other end without a subscription, so be aware! Most

CDs want to be able to download so they can edit into a package or pass onto directors and producers.

- There is more of a move for agents to be cut out from perusing the sides or the self-tape as a way for productions to sustain confidentiality. By business work ethic, it is an unwritten responsibility of any agent to keep all information confidential. Signing a Non-Disclosure Agreement (NDA) or not obtaining sides or not being able to give input to their client on a self-tape just doesn't make sense, particularly when the reader or camera person get to hear and see the whole lot without any signatures.

Grooming

Hair and face are the biggest issue as it is what is seen first. Hair needs to be washed and styled the day of the audition. Some can style their hair the day or week before and still have it immaculate but for the most part, bed hair might be sexy to a partner but not to a CD. Short hair may prove difficult during the pandemic as getting it professionally cut may not be an option with regional lockdowns and restrictions.

The only way round this is to use accessories, hair clips or hair gel to smooth out any imperfections or slightly change the style. A good option is for housemates or partners to practise on each other with a 'baby' trim. Nothing drastic, remember, more can be cut off though it can't be put back on. Practising on children is an option to start with as they don't seem to notice a bad haircut. It is worth investing in a professional pair of hair scissors, not to be used on anything else as it blunts the blades, very useful to tidy up bangs, and a pair of clippers for very short hair or to trim facial hair.

Colouring hair is a little bit more risky. Solid colour or bleeding in blocks of the colour when trying to streak or balayage takes a lot of practice, so is not recommended. Hair products sold in pharmacies are not professional so you may not get the desired lift in colour or bleach. Colouring to a lighter shade is EXTREMELY risky. Using spray on sun-kissed, gradual lightening type products that lighten your hair every time they are used are almost impossible for hairdressers to properly correct. It may seem like a reasonable decision at the time but could mean having to grow out for years and/or cut the hair short as the only solution.

For short periods, a good option to hide hair growth and grey hairs is to use magic temporary one-wash colour sprays to cover roots or dry shampoos with a hint of colour. If dark roots and wanting blonde, try the lightest colour on the market as most will turn the hair orange. During lockdown in the UK, all of the extra light spray in colour concealers were sold out for months. Presenters used dark hair wash in and out sprays for roots instead, hiding the grey to pretend that was their natural hair colour and growing out the blonde and this worked.

Use make up that you are used to. Having flawless-looking skin is key and thick foundations can look too heavy on HD self-tapes. Mixing a bit of foundation with moisturiser can reduce the heaviness but still provide enough coverage, or experiment with tinted moisturisers. Spray tans that look orange should be avoided, better to stay natural. Have a stock of suitable foundations which usually have long expiry dates and don't go out of fashion – the same with a bronzer, neutral but enhancing lipstick, eyeshadow and mascara. All are wise outlays considering the uncertainty of the pandemic.

Groomed eyebrows are a necessity, no monobrows, not too thin or extreme, just plucking a few odd hairs and using a clear brush solution or gel for eyebrows that keeps them in place. There are eyebrow brush colour solutions for slightly thinning and greying brows and are useful for anyone. Invest in a good pair of tweezers that will grip a single hair firmly and a magnifying mirror if required.

Nails should be neat, and the same length always looks well groomed. Keeping nails short will reduce the amount of germs that accumulate underneath the nail and make them easier to clean with soap and water, reducing transmission of the coronavirus. Do your own pale French manicure or keep plain and pale (low maintenance) and pushing the cuticles back. No loud nail colours, which when they chip look worse than no colour at all. Colour detracts from the performance unless this is part of the character you are trying to portray and is best avoided.

Finally waxing, shaving or other methods of hair removal, if required, might be something trialled before the day of audition, i.e. as to remove the hair without causing red blotching or irritation.

CHAPTER 8

COVID-19 Wardrobe Spring Clean

The fashion industry is keen on circularity, also known as a circular economy, which is focused on eliminating waste and the ongoing depletion of resources. The aim of this ideology is to get the longest use out of equipment and clothing. This is to an extent already in play in the entertainment industry by hiring, restoring and sharing, costumes, props and sets. Though can we take this to a more personal level?

Our generation has more clothes than ever before and has a disposable mentality. The cost of clothes more affordable with easily accessible bargains online that are eye candy and delivered straight to your door (more attractive in lockdown). Social media promotes peer pressure to be draped in new outfits on a regular basis.

What we should be doing and have forgotten to do is the **big spring clean**. Whilst stuck at home with less to do it's a perfect time for re-trying on, repairing and familiarising oneself with clothes that may have been forgotten. Then do a proper COVID-19 wardrobe spring clean culling clothing no longer useful or practical.

With government guidance requiring more isolation, stuck indoors at home more of the time and hence using more heating particularly in colder countries, provides a perfect breeding ground for starving moths who love dirty clothes and natural fabrics like silk, feathers, sheepskin and wool. More clothes mean more moth larvae, especially if the clothes are undisturbed for months at a time, like that little black dress or suit that you wore 10 years ago, cost a fortune, shabby and won't again fit, but sentimentally, something you can't offload.

During the pandemic, not working or socialising outside the home has meant we tend to wear the same old things to keep the good items in good condition for when we can get out again, choosing more comfortable options, unless you're in a new relationship at home and want to impress. Those that homeschooled didn't have time to worry about makeup and wardrobe.

Those vintage clothes and charity shops items or hand me downs mean you may be burying not just cheaper clothes but the moths that can come with them. This can happen with new clothes stacked in warehouses, less often, but it can happen with unused blankets stacked near clothes. The same with wool insulation, as we try to save the planet and go green, despite the environmental benefits, this is a perfect environment for the initiation and propagation of moths.

Checklist:
- If you haven't worn a garment in the past two years, it

may be unfashionable, although fashions come around again and knowing what suits you brings your own individuality. Perhaps it is time to give it to charity, sell if in good condition, or repair the item if that is why you haven't worn it. Sometimes we gain or lose weight, our body shape changes due to hormone changes, age or pregnancy, so be critical or ask a friend to help, what looks good and complements your figure. Will you really ever get back into that garment you're saving(?), are questions we need to ask ourselves.

- Use hot temperatures to wash clothes to kill moths, water needs to be at 60°C (140°F) or a high temperature tumble dry. Lots of clothes many shrink at this temperature so read the label. An alternative is to take garments to the dry cleaners or invest in a portable steam cleaner which may be paid off within three visits to the dry cleaners. Just as heating tongs kill hair lice, high heat kills moth larvae. Dust mites are killed by placing your pillow or blanket in a bag in the freezer for 24 hours, so too can moths be killed, so bag them and place in the freezer. A steamer is useful as it sanitises the clothes, particularly good for shared costumes during the pandemic and leaves the garment wrinkle free ready to put back on the hanger without washing. Less washing means less wear and tear to the garment so longer usage.

- Wash or steam second-hand clothes as pre-owned clothes and furniture need thorough vacuuming and washing at high temperatures, dry cleaning or steam cleaning.

- Pack away some precious keepsakes, like silk and woollens, to prevent moth larvae getting in – it will not eliminate moths but helps to prevent them devouring garments. Be wary of vacuum sealing as this breaks the fabric strands in garments making it hard to get out wrinkles. Keep the dirty bin outside and away from your precious clothes.

- Do a proper spring clean by moving furniture, cleaning and vacuuming everywhere under rugs, bedding, radiators, inside wardrobes, and then empty the vacuum cleaner so moths don't live inside there.

- Use of cedar wood or lavender in various products like moth balls helps to disguise the smell of any food left on garments or sweaty clothes, dissuading moths but not eliminating.

If you dry clean, take the plastic off the clothes when home as the plastic gives static to clothes nearby and attracts dust. There may also be, depending on the temperature, condensation and stains that might oxidise under the bag. When storing items, try using acid free tissue and rolling the garments to avoid creasing.

If you can't see what you have in your cupboard, or if it doesn't complement your current figure, for it is important for self-tapes to have clothes that fit properly, then it is time to rehome the garment. It's time to re-assess your colour and style, as you change, physically and with age, the colours and cuts will change. You can wear any colour but need to work out what season you are, autumn colours or blue-based or yellow-based colours, so the tones are important to work out whether you need warm or cold colours to pop. This is a time to go through your wardrobe and look at your colour palate, put on your clothes and see what fits you, be realistic about where you will be physically in four months and long term.

CHAPTER 9

Rising Up Through COVID-19

An artist requires a wide range of skills which may include emotional aptitude, a mature imagination, vocal projection, clarity of speech, spatial awareness, physicality, musicality, ability to perform various dialects and accents, display different body language, improvisation, observe and mimic, mime, comedic, and stage combat.

There are also other skills that would enable an artist to be more employable. Obtaining a Master's degree seems an inviting option to artists when work seems slow, though unless a scholarship is granted, the financial costs for the course as well as supporting a lifestyle may be overwhelming weighted against the gains. In the UK, there are reputable masters courses, e.g., in Musical Theatre at the Royal Academy of Arts (RAM) that hold great esteem in the industry and help to retrain actors whose undergraduate degree was not focused in this area. This is a viable reason to develop and hone skills at an advanced level. If a performer is interested in academia, gaining a Master's though having limited practical experience, i.e. impressive professional credits, is likely to be of insufficient standard.

Within the arts, academic roles tend to require a proven track record of excellence in industry and/or published papers in reputable journals and/or postgraduate studies that require independent driven research (e.g., PhD). Unfortunately, universities are no longer just educators, they are a business and providing a one-year additional masters (by course work) which commands a good fee from students, helps to service their profits.

Additional qualifications, beyond drama training or a related degree, rarely supersede the experience on the shop floor when it comes to the entertainment industry and this is what CDs are looking for. However, additional skills may be helpful on a personal level, e.g. editing courses, to cut and chop, re-order show reels and this is appealing to CDs for recruiting actors who can put the whole package together for UGC, particularly during a lockdown.

Artists can peruse through the options of accents/dialects, languages, skills, etc., on casting portholes where they have uploaded their CV and already filled out their current talents, as a way of getting ideas. Getting a driving licence is a good investment. Much less requested, in descending order, is a licence for motorcycles, trucks/lorries, scuba diving, firearms and boats. There has been the obscure request, namely a taxi/cab, tractor or forklift licence. For car commercials, a driving licence is mandatory for insurance purposes if the car is active.

Artists living in big cities might find it too congested to drive and easier to get around via public transport, and shy away from obtaining a driving licence. Though the number of times a client has missed out on a well paid advertisement contract or a top role on screen, that required a full driving licence, also needs to be 'clean': so no fines; is more common than not. During the pandemic, a licence provides additional personal benefits in the work environment. Instead of unit cars, the artist has the flexibility to use a personal hire car from the airport and for the duration of the shoot. A licence is convenient, for picking up groceries, in getting to set and reducing social interactions. Then there are the productions that are filmed remotely – having a licence may mean greater flexibility and autonomy even if not requiring the licence for the job directly. Study of the rules of the road can be done remotely. Obviously practicing behind the wheel and the practical exam is an issue due to pandemic implications, though an artist can be ready to go as soon as things improve.

Stage combat is useful, as is dance of any kind, and at any level, e.g. ballroom, tap, ballet, acrobatics comes up, as does juggling on the odd occasion. In terms of sport, yoga, snow skiing, swimming (face under water), off shore swiming, cycling, parkour, skate boarding, ice skating, inline skating, seem more frequent than others.

Musical theatre requires artists to be a triple threat (unless 'name') to have the best opportunities and having a portable instrument for any artist comes into use when CDs are doubling up on musician/roles for production to keep costs down. It is a desirable skill, more so than ever, due to social distancing measures, having the musicians as part of the ensemble rather than as an addition. All this will depend on the style of production, whether period or contemporary. Re-visiting an instrument played during childhood is the obvious option, particularly if it is portable. Instruments more commonly asked for, in descending order, are guitar (electric or acoustic), drums, violin, woodwind, brass, accordion, ukulele, piano/keyboards, bass guitar and harmonica.

Singing as a featured artist, whether it is choral, lead rock, opera (great if able to read music), is more useful for theatre or live events though occasionally pops up in films or commercials. Lockdown and restricted private teaching due to social interaction concerns has led to numerous resources and classes available online for the budding and experienced musician and singer. Singing scale warmups found online, many that are free – even practising for just 15 minutes a day will make a difference, as the voice is an instrument that needs to be practised regularly. Build it into a routine then it becomes an integral part of your life. Try building up a repertoire of contrasting songs, spend an hour each day when possible and choose material for roles that you would legitimately be cast for and is within your register and style of singing.

Online learning for instruments is varied, affordable and there is a huge selection, though it is worth doing a trial, as a video telephony one-on-one style of teaching may be more favourable. Remembering that any instrument utilising the mouth/breath, including singing may not be as popular in as many productions during COVID-19, due to possibly spreading the virus over further distances, though it is still a good time to practise any instrument for future use.

In the earlier days in the USA blockbusters filmed in Europe, the lead or A-list actors were flown out from the USA, the B-list or supporting actors mostly taken from the UK as native English speakers and the rest of the cast selected on location, e.g., Berlin, Germany, because of the number of American accented actors located there and perhaps filming incentives and tax breaks. As part of a brief, CDs request artists who have certain language skills and specific accents but in general they want native speakers, usually based in the country where the production company is based or where the set will be located. It doesn't mean having a second language is of no use, as if filming with a director or in another country, then the artist being proficient in the language of that country may be an added bonus on set.

If an artist is bilingual, they should know the region of the accent for the language, e.g., if English, then is it, for example,

Mancuniuan or Liverpudlian, if Italian, is it Milanese or Neapolitan, if French is it Parisienne or Provençal, if Arabic is it Egyptian or Saudi etc. Agents will not necessarily be able to distinguish the nuances of dialects and accents from all regions so artists need to educate their agent and be honest as to whether it is spoken as a native or as a foreigner (any self-tape submissions will go to those who can recognise native speakers for assessment thus best not to pretend, in fact, detrimental to do so for any potential future work).

This is imperative when it comes to VO, stating the obvious which is sometimes not fully appreciated, the voice is the main and only focus and any imperfections become blatantly obvious, very quickly. With regional accents, researching the accent and performing on stage over a short period of months may not mean an artist is automatically native! I can always look at an artist and hone in on their mannerisms, and decide if it is believable, if the voice matches the body language. It is not just the dialect/accent but understanding the demeanour and background, the slight inflexions and nuances. Artists who live in the region for some years, tend to be able to learn the dialect not just the accent, and mimic the mannerisms naturally.

Other forms of communication might be avenues for an artist to expand on, like languages that are inaudible. There are approximately 135 different languages in sign language, that can be learnt, and British Sign Language (BSL) is not the same as Australian Sign Language (Auslan) and not the same as American Sign Language (ASL) so this is like a dialect and needs to reflect the region that an artist is living and/or working in for the skill to be marketable.

I will never forget a client in my first year as an agent, who called after an audition and gave me a good talking to - because I had not explained they would be told to do the sides in another accent. I was somewhat taken a back. CDs or directors can ask for the sides to be done in a slightly different manner which includes the accent, this isn't something they would necessarily go through before the casting and very much dependant on the day of audition. They might see the artist in another role rather than the one put up for or think the performer might feel more natural with a different accent. I asked my British artist who had grown up in London (for the most part), "what accent did they spring on you?". The reply was, "They wanted a Cockney accent, I can do London and RP (Received Pronunciation) but not a Cockney". I couldn't believe this, it wasn't as if the CD was asking for a Yupik accent. It was as if they had never heard the accent, despite being London based and coming across the accent in normal life and brought up on national TV, so soaps like Eastenders. The client should have given the accent a go and probably would have done OK. Instead their reluctance demonstrated a resistance to being flexible, a limit in range and reaffirmation of the artist's insecurities.

Artists usually spend more time out of entertainment work, than in work, even if glowing credits so the money in most cases, tends to be tight. There is nothing worse than the desperate artist, the one that is hassling the agent for work with unnecessary weekly calls, "what's the market like?", "did I get a callback?", or "when do you think we'll know?". Unfortunately CDs don't have the luxury to ring round and provide feedback to agents anymore, nor do they do many 'generals' where they would see artists for a chat over coffee. Normally, if the agent has not contacted the client within a week for commercials, perhaps a little longer for film and TV depending on the shoot dates (which has been more influenced and fluid due to COVID-19 rescheduling issues), and maybe two weeks for stage, then the role is probably not on the cards.

However, very rarely, there are last minute calls, perhaps because a lead on set couldn't get out of bed and the agent/client hadn't heard anything for months till that day of shoot, and the agent is madly negotiating the contract and the artist learning lines before stepping on set that very same morning!

There seems to be some crazy advice floating around the web, that during COVID-19, this is a time to phone and pitch yourself to CDs and productions. This is definitely not one of those times. Businesses are trying to survive and uncertain of what work they can continue with or do in the future, so they have bigger problems then talking to an artist who is so desperate for work and whom they have never heard of before.

Managing money is particularly challenging during the virus and a struggle for most artists at the best of times. This is a balance that is often not taught at drama schools when it affects the life of an artist so profoundly. Money is required to pay for the essentials, e.g. travel to a recall, grooming, clothes for auditions and the ability to afford the tools for the trade like the acting directory/casting platforms, show reel, headshots etc. Having more money at the end of the day or week left after all the outgoings/expenses, then this suggests that the money is being budgeted and properly managed.

I've meet plenty of top actors who don't realise the burden the business has on them once they have a family, the commitment to raising a child (children) not only does it put demands on time and money, but there are frequent last minute hiccups to manoeuvre, simply things like leaving the house could take another 15 minutes and that's the easy part. Some artists end up so busy trying to provide for the family that performance can no longer be the main focus, attracted to more secure acting jobs such as role play long term contracts for government bodies and before you know it, years have passed and the CV has very few professional current roles.

Artists are creative by nature and a proportion have, undoubtedly, hidden writing talents. It has been proven that performers can create their own destiny, develop a script that casts them in the perfect lead role, e.g. Ben Affleck in 'Good Will Hunting', or Ricky Gervais in 'The Office'. This has been a way in for artists to make their fortune and it seems a natural progression for well-known and/or experienced artists to transverse into directing and/or producing roles.

One-person shows are not a good investment when unknown or not a comedian. One artist I advised, was going through a fertility program with their partner, they had amazing credits but pointed out that their elevated height may be an issue on certain productions, e.g. the stage production of Mousetrap, where all of the actors need to be around 5'7 so that the audience can't guess who the murderer is. This holds true for any stage or screen casting, if the leads are 5'2, having an artist towering over at 6'4 will portray a different character/story/feel (and technically, hard to get the right camera shots). Though the notion of writing, producing and acting (the money and time and pressure) to produce a one hander show was unlikely to attract CDs who were generally busy, and more interested in utilising their talent scout time by seeing a group of artists. The other problem is one-person shows tend to run for hours, rarely enticing. The artist's main aim was to obtain further acting work, not to showcase their skills as a writer or producer. Instead, the better option was to write to a select few, research CDs and directors who have worked with taller actors, who have worked on action based narratives (as the artist's credits were strong in this area) and supply them an easy click link of their show reel/CV - which were so impressive, this to me was enough to sell them, but it needed to get to the right people. This was where they had been going wrong for many years, they were focusing on getting to CDs, any CD, but not realising which were the ones they should target and reach out to based on their characteristics and abilities.

There are a lot of writing classes out there, but artists can learn by doing, by reading scripts and then watching the production if possible, and vice versa. And identifying their USP, this enables an artist to pigeonhole the CDs to reach out to.

Representation

'My agent doesn't get me any work', is one of the most common excuses artists seek new representation. Performance is one of the most competitive industries known, unlike 'conventional' professions, even when you are a fantastic artist and good at your job, that doesn't mean the role will be offered. Briefs mean that productions require performers with a certain accent or language, talent, colouring, build, personality, or have a certain amount of experience. Agents can only get performers work if the role is out there and they are on brief.

The virus has meant there is less work, many a production suspended, the few scrambling to reshoot in attempt to complete the film or series, others closed down until further notice or undecided if the project is a feasible financial possibility. There seems no point in opening up theatres or starting new productions. The industry, mainstream, hangs on 'bums on seats', 'names', international and social presence and this has always been the case.

Hundreds of agencies exist in cities in the USA, UK, and Europe. Countries, such as China, do not have an agency culture hence production communicate direct with an artist. SAG-AFTRA (Screen Actors Guild and the American Federation of Television and Radio Artists) represents approximately 160,000 performers and this includes everyone associated with screen entertainment i.e., actors, announcers, broadcast journalists, dancers, DJs, news writers, news editors, program hosts, puppeteers, recording artists, singers, stunt performers, voiceover artists and other media professionals. Equity is the UK trade union that represents performers and other artists working across the live and recorded entertainment industry with over 45,000 members.

Finding an agent or changing agencies during the pandemic is more difficult than ever. Any agency does not have the power to guarantee work or auditions, this is the prerogative of production companies, the producers and CDs that they use. It takes time for agencies to know their clients and the higher number they have, and depending on resources, the less they know about their clients and less able to suggest them appropriately for the right work.

Asking fellow artists on their feelings towards their current agent is a useful way to start researching, but be aware, not all will be willing to share their agent with you if they are great and if you are of a similar disposition (you're competition!) –

they will be less likely to provide a glowing recommendation. Other artists may be unhappy with any agent, playing the blame game for not getting roles and jumping from one to the next.

A client introduced me to a disgruntled fellow artist, who had impressive credits and would be a fine addition to the books, as I had no-one similar. We set up an interview. The artist and I reviewed their show reel, photos and CV, which were of high standard and discussed what auditions and CDs they had met. They were getting seen for top quality work and that they were on brief for. The fact that the auditions were not converting to the number of jobs they expected was in no way a reflection on the abilities of their agent. The number of castings was low but as with any business, there are different cycles and the artist just wasn't the flavour of the month (or year as it seemed). I didn't know their agent but recommended they stay put, as the agent was doing a great job and I didn't think I could do any better. What it did show, was an unhappy artist irrespective of the hard work of their agent. "It's the fish that

John West Rejects that makes John West the best.", is what sprang to mind. It is all about professionalism, commitment, timing and not just talent.

When a drama school tries to sell graduate students because they fit the current trend, irrespective of the reputation of the school and high level of teaching, if they can't act, then any good agent wouldn't be interested. Though if they are on the cusp of being able to act, being on trend is clearly an advantage and will push them into favour .

If unable to gain suitable recommendations, then start with state or country directories of agencies which exist via most performing arts portholes. Working out those that are within the same city or region is helpful for future face-to-face contact and same time zone interactions. When researching locations and types of agents (which can be a formidable task as the number listed can be staggering!) perhaps starting from 'Z' and working back to 'A' when researching the agencies, rather than the conventional A to Z which does not necessary mean the name in chronological order represents a better agent. Be careful of out-of-date websites that rank agencies or CDs that are obsolete and have no substance or credibility though claim to. Deciding on whether they have an unmanageably large portfolio, the type of work, location and style of clients, gives an artist an idea as to whether they might be a good fit.

Reviews on social media platforms are not the best indicator as a disgruntled artist whose pride has been damaged can provide unprofessional evaluation, or larger companies have the ability to request removal of comments from search engines and sites that they might find damaging, even if they are true.

Agencies differ greatly in their company ethos – some will work whatever hours required for their client and answer emails that are urgent over the weekend for last minute castings, particularly if an international casting, so different overseas time zones or self-tapes, whilst others obey a strict weekday from 9am (or 10am) to 6pm Monday to Friday.

Artists should refrain from contacting their agents on weekends or after hours unless urgent, e.g., problems on set or illness so can't attend a flight for a job.

Different individual agents will have a spectrum of styles, those with fewer clients perhaps offering a more one-on-one personal management approach (unless there is a legal distinction between agent and manager responsibilities as it exists in some countries like the USA), guiding the artist more closely in their career not just pushing the client forward for just any paid work.

Any good agent should know the basics about their artist e.g., height, languages, skills, credits, if they have pets and children, availability, (sometimes a confidant for their personal life) and hence can answer CDs enquiries immediately without having to search through the archive. This aids the agent, finding the artist suitable auditions, working on quality and not quantity, which increases the hit rate and allows the artist to be seen by the CD at their best.

Any reputable agent works on commissions, not charging upfront fees to join or being attached to photographers – they only make money when the clients earns. When you are an up-and-coming star, beware of the agent who coincidentally turns up at your local yoga lesson, or bumps into you at stage door, who promises to brand you, offering cutting edge marketing techniques, name dropping and discussing opportunities (roles not yet locked in, or made up) which your current agent has missed for you. Some agencies are great marketers (of themselves), and prey upon the insecurities and uncertainty of the artist, claiming they can accelerate the artist's career and do better than anyone else, though this is normally not the case. Clients approached in this manner have, the majority of the time, left a competent agent, mislead that the grass is greener on the other side, and some years later the progress is evident that changing to the 'new' agency was a dire decision.

If your current agent has made good headway with your career and you trust them, they are reputable and most importantly honest, it is a worthy partnership. Artists need to have faith their agent is doing their job as that will allow the performer to get on with the job of acting. Don't be mesmerised by the big firms, who brag they have all the contacts. They might have ten similar artists to suggest for the same role, which means the agency relies more heavily on their assistants or secretaries in suggesting clients on briefs, or the agency may be too busy answering the calls of celebrity clients, pre-occupied with their career progression – and less time to focus on emerging talent when the novelty of CDs to meet that 'new talent' again wears off.

One can make the analogy of buying a product as being similar to that of booking an artist, the CD (is the buyer) who would purchase that product from the smaller retailer (agency) especially if the agent (the seller) can tell the CD exactly why the artist is perfect for the role, instantly know their availability and all the ins and outs offering a more personalised and efficient service. If the artist is good and the agency reputable, there is no reason why talent wouldn't be contracted via smaller boutique agencies.

Maintaining a solid relationship with your agent means dealing with them professionally, in the same manner within the partnership as it existed prior to COVID-19. This is not the time to be calling your agent asking what work there is - the facts are, there is very little good quality work, the situation is fluid and productions have location and set issues surrounding filming and stage, or other live events severely restricted with government guidance. Logistically, getting actors on set or on stage for a performance from another region or country has its own problems that are difficult to factor in due to quarantine and travel factors.

It is not the best time to be switching or finding new representation. It takes time to know new clients, which not all agencies have, struggling to find work for those currently on their books. Social distancing means artists cannot be properly interviewed at length in the office or seen performing. Though some agencies may disagree with this, depending on the work they source, and may welcome new clients, exploring the possibilities with the artist via video telephony and satisfied with viewing existing show reel material. They may ask for an audition self-tape.

Perusing the agencies websites will give an indication as to whether to apply and their preferences for receiving submissions. When agencies have a clear message that they are not taking on new talent, they do mean their books are closed. There is no point emailing or writing to them expressing interest. Maybe focus on the relationship that already exists and help your current agent, i.e. by updating the CV, show reel, VO, making sure the headshot is current (when possible), compiling a list of CDs visited, maybe a spreadsheet including the dates, production name, a short summary of the event, and any learnt lessons. Or a list of CDs you would like to work with and why. Do your research – on the world wide web there are numerous interviews with top international CDs that can provide great insight to the budding artist. This data will be helpful for your agent as well as for reflection within.

Reconnect with CDs, directors and producers that know you and particularly during COVID-19, it needs to be personal. Being proactive may mean to '**do less more often**', or a compound effect where 10 minutes a day over a period of time, could make significant change, or there is the ripple effect where one small change can propagate into many other changes, almost a knock on effect not too dissimilar to the butterfly effect.

Start with small manageable objectives, even one thing each day and strive for consistency. For instance, an artist could pick five CDs and ADs and write to them every six months or so, post-COVID-19 maybe an update on the artist's work, or provide an opinion on the director's or CD's latest production (keep it positive!), or the artist could supply an updated headshot link: having a genuine reason as to why the artist is making contact helps. Again, this requires a list that the artist can go back to, narrowing it down, choosing theatres that are within the vicinity of the artist, an additional reason for interest in the venue due to reduced travel time and accessibility, and familiarity with the style of production or in the director, who may share similar values.

Some professionals have ample time to read with less work and are happy to have a sunny postcard or note updating them of new headshots, or personal experiences of lockdown, or perhaps what the artist has been doing to upskill. The idea is to make sure that, if you contact a CD or AD, the note is sincere, short and sweet. Don't assume that they have shared the same experience, so be careful and considerate of the terminology used.

I received an email after lockdown from an artist seeking representation, starting with, "I'm sure you had a great summer….", then going on with phrases like, "has been a great experience" and "have enjoyed the time to read". I thought, it wasn't a great summer at all stuck indoors and the economy plummeting, it was an experience but I wouldn't define it as 'great' and am very pleased that you had time to read and enjoyed it, though I had no spare time having to multi-task so we are not on the same wavelength. Then I hit the 'DELETE' button, involuntarily… A better way to start might be something along the lines of, "I hope you are doing well.". Maybe during this sensitive period, approaching those in the business may require more intensive research or being mindful of others, before shooting off an email or letter.

CHAPTER 10

Moving Forward

Well-known theatre establishments in the UK like the West End, The National Theatre, the Royal Shakespeare Company and The Globe are on hold, unable to offer social distancing as an economically viable option, so opening in 2021. Those venues that are opening in 2020 are, in general, open air theatres or productions with reduced numbers of artists that can follow government guidelines. Broadway New York, USA, has suspended all productions until January 2021, as has Friedrichstadt-Palast which is owned by the State of Berlin, Germany. Businesses cannot deal with uncertainty and until there is clear guidance, not just in the UK, but all over the world, or a vaccine that has longevity, the impact on the entertainment industries and as a consequence, on artists, could potentially last for the next three to five years. And even if we move beyond this pandemic in the near future, it is likely there will be other new deadly viruses to deal with.

It is still unclear as to what amount or density of viral particles it takes to infect a person. Living with and coping, as opposed to exterminating the virus to survive, one can only assume that everyone has COVID-19 and protect ourselves and each other. Asymptomatic can still be potentially highly contagious - the main reason the virus is so hard to control and monitor. In general, human beings (unconsciously in most cases, due to a lack of understanding or accountability), have poor hygiene, and this virus requires a very high level of attention to detail in order to control the spread.

The herd immunity philosophy may prove, from initial studies, to be futile as some groups have shown no immunity even just weeks after proving positive to testing, others only a matter of months. COVID-19 is proving to be a parallel and almost alien world for artists, as naturally social distancing measures and facial coverings, are not supportive of their need for physical expression and interaction in telling their intimate stories.

There are some useful lessons learned from COVID-19, some positive environmental implications, mindful hygiene regimes and social distancing may help to reduce the spread of viruses now and in the future. Society has had to adopt different working practises that may be better for the environment over time if we reduce the amount of pollution caused by long distance travel and reduce the volume of people having to travel. Encouraging employees to work from home remotely, using online communications and shared workspaces that are routinely disinfected and providing crews with their own personalised portable devices to take to and from work, all to facilitate reducing the use of resources.

Utensils that are disposable but made from recycled products already exist. These products reduce waste using already available edible cups made from seaweed, algae or cellulose that are based on plant polysaccharides though this requires chemical cross-linking which is moderately biodegradable. Currently in development is the use of plant proteins, (e.g., pea or potato) for micro plastics, that do not have a chemical cross-linking and thus can decompose rapidly and entirely within nature. Proteins are able to self-assemble and exist in a different form, similar to frying an egg, the clear liquid turns white, the protein of a pea can be fabricated into a sheet resembling a plastic film for use on sandwich packaging or to cover an apple, and totally edible.

Production on set will lean more towards the use of technology, more screens, larger screens rather than shared monitors, fewer people, microphone instructions rather than directly shouting to each other to avoid the spread of the virus and perhaps better and novel ways in communicating. Voice activated technologies and AI will develop, to avoid touching the screen of devices including cameras.

COVID-19 has sped up innovative ways of thinking in the

entertainment industries. There are many more start-ups developing AR, VR, XR and AI. XR smart glasses may be used to detect the spatial presence of a person within the real environment, with face recognition and location (better would be to then report this information via audio, a useful feature that could be adapted to social distancing, for example, by sounding an alarm if too close to others).

VR is also an exceptional educational tool, by allowing the participants to be involved, heightening learning, though there is no substitute for shared experience and multi-sensory absorption. Human beings want to experience events in 'real life' and this is where XR may come into play. Currently, VR does not offer the social experience most would expect but it does offer alternatives to conventional narration. Immersive storytelling falls short of providing the haptic, olfactory and visual experience. It looks unlikely that VR will replace live event; the tribal scents, the tiny nuances, the favourite t-shirt worn to a live event, the shouting out requests or laughing with that special friend beside us or the interaction with the performer and transporting us to a different place.

Distanced VR can be engaging but a distanced live gig doesn't engage – perhaps new reality technologies will be an additional component, not a replacement. Juxtaposition, maybe. It could be that VR may be an antidote for loneliness and provide an uplift in optimism for those that are isolated. However there is huge potential, as traditional gala productions can only accommodate a limited capacity due to the pandemic yet VR galas allows for endless viewers to tune in, though it is not cost affective at this time for the masses.

AR is a more accessible technology for the arts to be enjoyed and can reach more people. The most interesting areas are: virtual sets to avoid travel overseas and accommodating for any COVID-19 travel restrictions; green screen to mimic large crowds, minimising social contact; and, an option for reducing the waste of costume changes on stage by viewing through XR glasses. As little dolls were couriered between France and England in the 1800s to show samples of fabrics and designs, prototypes of adult sized garment, so too can VR or AR be used to superimpose the garment onto the bearer without physically having the costume at hand.

Artists can have dress rehearsals in VR or AR in times of distancing, or influencers can use an online library of fashion pieces to dress themselves for selfie shots for social branding online as opposed to ordering a new physical garment every time, hence supporting the environment.

There has been a huge digital change and the entertainment industry is embracing that change, adapting to the new environment by pivoting. Artists will think twice before boarding a plane to deal with an agent in another country and opt for the eco-friendly path by doing most of the preparation and rehearsals via video telephony. Online meetings has, in some ways, allowed for more lines of connection with no pretence – an authentic way of interacting with the top influencers whilst they clutch a cup of coffee from their home; a personal experience with the artist rather than in a fast paced city office.

Performers, particularly those in the music industry have developed closer relationships with their audience via technical industry streaming, digital campaigns and online social media sharing platforms, allowing artists more control over their artistic expression. Though this move to using technologically advanced home studios and branding is unlikely to make the big studios and agencies redundant. To be a megastar, an artist requires ongoing input from the best advisors, which large production companies tend to attract, as well as maintaining their international presence by continuous branding, all of this requires a machine behind them.

It is unlikely that governments will offer an insurance type product, such as that currently exists for terrorism for some productions. Unfortunately, with COVID-19, policies will not resemble the typical insurance model as individual productions are all being affected by the virus directly or indirectly at the same time. As projects have restarted, the scheduling of performers are 'considered' on a first call basis. Yet at the same time, are required on other restarting projects, globally, again as first call. A completion bond assumes that only parts of the production will be affected at any time, hence going forward, production companies are likely to require their own contingency funds.

This suggests the studios that are likely to function during coronavirus are those that can absorb costs due to other revenue streams e.g., Disney[+] on SVOD (subscription-based video-on-demand) or TVOD (transactional video-on-demand). Small production companies with fewer employees and contractors, will lower overheads that allow quick turnarounds are likely to survive. Medium to larger sized independent production companies may be impacted more severely financially due to the risks of COVID-19 infecting and isolating staff, thus rendering them unable to fulfil their job description yet still needing cover to fill the void. Substantial costs associated with several crew quarantined at the same time and the use of larger office spaces mean higher commercial rents, despite the space not being in use.

The distancing of performers, particularly in orchestras that utilise plastic screens between musicians, during the pandemic makes time delays an issue, and is the reason video telephony isn't useful for musical rehearsals. Rather than attending an event, audiences, particularly the younger groups, can stream content of performances, both international and homegrown, from international institutes such as: the Opera Zurich, Switzerland, The Bolshoi Theatre, Russia, San Francisco Dance Film Festival, USA, Cheltenham Literature Festival, UK, Norwegian National and view interviews with artists.

This is the birth of new streaming platforms that are targeted at arts and culture fans. During lockdowns there is an issue for live events, particularly those requiring large numbers of artists congregating together such as opera and orchestras. Perhaps the face and mouth shield visor with adjustable anti-fog, anti-saliva, options that are both breathable and washable can be slightly modified and shaped more intricately over the contours of the artist. This mimics the ideas of the ancient Greeks, circa 400 BC, where two masks associated with ancient Greek drama were the smiling face, representing Comedy, and the frowning countenance, representing Tragedy, can be modernised and adopted.

Pre-COVID-19 there was a move by Hollywood away from blockbuster films to producing content for SVOD, as a more cost effective and efficient way to turn out new projects. Content is being shown on several platforms, and it is content overload though it is cumbersome for finding productions of interest. It may result in dismissing in-house productions despite the use of big 'names' because of the lack of good scripts or style.

During the pandemic audience viewing numbers on SVOD exploded and hopefully the additional revenue obtained by production houses will provide better funding to support unique and appealing projects in the aftermath as well as a more satisfactory audience viewing experience. Over the next few years self-content creation will become more popular as it has the advantage of social distancing, a personal aspect and reduced outlay.

Avoiding infection from COVID-19 may be due to the lack of prevalence as opposed to society's impeccable hygiene standards. A single cough can produce thousands of droplets that end up on clothing and other surfaces and smaller particles can remain in the air. It is suggested that the virus is shed long before symptoms and lingers in faecal matter. Shared toilets seem a particular hazard zone when people don't adequately wash their hands and can contaminate surfaces they touch. There is a real need for hand sanitiser application training on set for cast and crew. UV lights can be used to test surfaces for substances such as urine and bacteria to fluoresce and which the naked eye would not normally detect. Just as healthcare and food service locations use imaging technologies to make the invisible visible, so should productions to aid in COVID-19 health and safety measures.

Using alternatives to current stainless steel tapes/faucets, e.g. copper (Cu) alloys like bronze (Cu with tin) and brass (Cu with zinc) should be implemented for the future as COVID-19 survives on glass and stainless steel for days but on copper, is inactive in hours. Any microbe that comes in contact with copper ions (so interacts with the 'lonely' free electron in the outer orbital shell of the Cu atom), will attack the germ by breaking the cell membrane or, as with COVID-19, the viral coating which then initiates free radicals that speed up the process for deactivating the virus. Useful in not encouraging drug-resistant superbugs (that occur by mutation), the copper ions target DNA and RNA inside the virus or bacteria. Even when copper becomes a light green and tarnishes, the beneficial properties are not compromised. Copper alloys should be used more in our workplaces, hospitals and public transport, and on set. On chair armrests, door handles, bathroom accessories etc., though copper is a conductor and the usage hence needs to be carefully considered.

Autonomous robots have a useful purpose during COVID-19

to disinfect surfaces outside office hours to reduce toxic exposure for cleaning staff, cast and crew. This is particularly of use to reduce exposure of chemicals by those more susceptible to irritants found in liquid disinfectants, supplying additional periods of time where the space can be properly ventilated before production resumes.

There are robots being tested that use short-wavelength UV light to deactivate viruses, a process known as ultraviolet germicidal irradiation, though as yet not 100% efficient in tackling the virus. Human intervention is required for hard to reach areas such as door handles or point of service technologies. This may reduce the reliance on the number and regularity of cleaning staff that may be travelling from various production sites and cross contaminating without knowing. It is often postulated that the virus spreads from the toilets to the canteen when cleaners use the same gloves and cleaning sponges. PPE should be changed at every location.

Evidence suggest vitamin D levels play an important part in

combating the disease hence levels can be checked with a physician and options discussed. Levels below 70 ng/mL may indicate a deficiency which is not uncommon during autumn and winter months in countries like the UK and those outside the Tropics of Capricorn and Cancer. People who have little to no sunlight exposure, e.g. shielding or self-isolating, should consider taking a vitamin D supplement all year round.

NICE (National Institute for Care and Health Excellence) has found no correlation for whether or not vitamin D helps with any respiratory diseases including COVID-19. Although the lack of vitamin D contributes to fatigue, muscle weakness and aches or cramps and mood changes like depression, which the latter seems more prevalent during this pandemic period and worth addressing in any event.

Effective testing regimes are the only way forward to minimise the spread of the virus. The scientific evidence has yet to confirm whether SARS-CoV-2 antibodies can protect from reinfection or how long those antibodies persist, so a vaccine may not be fit for all purpose.

Modification of our everyday lives due to the pandemic is sometimes referred to as the 'new normal', though there is nothing normal about it. What we do know is that this is pivotal time in our lives where we must adopt, cope and soldier on.

To rehash, don't touch your face, wear a mask when required, organise your meetings outside in a well ventilated environment, stay at home as much as possible, restrict social physical contact by keeping a decent distance, maintain a healthy weight and prioritise and address medical concerns. Virologists believe time of exposure is a major factor in contracting the virus, with minimal risk if a brief 'Hi' to a friend in the street rather than choosing a sit down for lunch with a friend for hours, which is at the other end of the spectrum – perhaps a quick coffee outside and distanced is a more sensible option.

Eating healthy foods and keeping fitness levels up by incorporating exercise into the daily routine, which might be walking up and down stairs (bypassing the elevator where possible not only for fitness but also reducing confined aerosol risk, virus particles on buttons and close personal contact) or many small fast walks or runs during the day, perhaps singing for lung exercises, strengthen the diaphragm to aid in breathing if compromised due to virus.

On some days it is hard to get out of bed, or easy to feel depressed, or we may feel unmotivated towards work, particularly with the hardships we are facing during the pandemic. Again, there is a spectrum of experience and on my bad days as a twenty year old I would nonchalantly chant, 'another day, another dollar' and that would motivate me enough to get on with the day despite dreading to be back in the office. I had a poster illustrating light blue skies, fluffy clouds and sun beams, that continues to resonate with me today, which read, 'Every day is a new beginning'.

Stay positive, be resilient. BE STRONG. You are GREAT. Nothing is forever, nor is this pandemic. Common sense approaches to one's health, use of technological advances and dogged determination on the part of the production crews and artists can ensure that 'the show must go on' and it will.

Printed in Poland
by Amazon Fulfillment
Poland Sp. z o.o., Wrocław